THE JOURNAL JURISPRUDENCE

VOLUME FOUR

"THE JURISPRUDENCE OF TORTS"

Contributors

Ms. Brooke Glass-O'Shea
University of Southern California

Mr Jonathan Blackmore
Shepard Broad Law Center
Nova Southeastern University

Associate Professor Robert L. McFarland
Faulkner University

Mr Josh Masters
New York University

Editor

Mr Aron Ping D'Souza
University of Melbourne

MICHAELMAS TERM
OCTOBER 2009

Elias Clark

PUBLISHED BY THE ELIAS CLARK GROUP

DISTRIBUTED IN CONNECTION WITH THE GALE GROUP,
A PART OF CENGAGE LEARNING

The Elias Clark Group
www.elias-clark.com

GPO Box 5001
Melbourne, Victoria 3001
Australia

First Published 2009.

Cataloguing-in-Publication entry

Editor:	D'Souza, Aron Ping.
Authors:	D'Souza, Aron Ping. Glass-O'Shea, Brooke. Blackmore, Jonathan. McFarland, Robert L. Masters, Josh.
Title:	The Journal Jurisprudence, Volume Four, "The Jurisprudence of Torts."
ISBN:	978-0-9807318-1-1 (pbk.)
ISSN:	1836-0955
Subjects:	Law – jurisprudence. Philosophy –general.

This edition may be cited as

(2009) J. Juris.

followed by the page number

ABOUT THE TYPEFACE

The Journal Jurisprudence is typeset in Garamond 12 and the footnotes are set in Garamond 10. The typeface was named for Claude Garamond (c. 1480 - 1561) and are based on the work of Jean Jannon. By 1540, Garamond became a popular choice in the books of the French imperial court, particularly under King Francis I. Garamond was said to be based on the handwriting of Angelo Vergecio, a librarian to the King. The italics of Garamond are credited to Robert Grandjon, an assistant to Claude Garamond. The font was re-popularised in the art deco era and became a mainstay on twentieth-century publication. In the 1970s, the font was redesigned by the International Typeface Corporation, which forms the basis of the variant of Garamond used in this Journal.

TABLE OF CONTENTS

CALL FOR PAPERS

The field of jurisprudence lies at the nexus of law and politics, the practical and the philosophical. By understanding the theoretical foundations of law, jurisprudence can inform us of the place of legal structures within larger philosophical frameworks. In its inaugural edition, *The Journal Jurisprudence* received many creative and telling answers to the question, "What is Law?" For the second edition, the editors challenged the scholarly and lay communities to inquire into intersection between jurisprudence and economics.

With the backing of our diverse and disparate community, *The Journal Jurisprudence* has now evolved into a more diverse form. We will no longer be setting a question for each issue, but instead designing issues around the articles we received. Therefore, we invite scholars, lawyers, judges, philosophers and lay people tackle the any and all of the great questions of law. Knowing that ideas come in all forms, papers can be of any length, although emphasis is placed on readability by lay audiences.

Papers may engage with case studies, philosophical arguments or any other method that answers philosophical question applicable to the law. Importantly, articles will be selected based upon quality and the readability of works by non-specialists. The intent of the Journal is to involve non-scholars in the important debates of legal philosophy.

The Journal also welcomes and encourages submissions of articles typically not found in law journals, including opinionated or personalised insights into the philosophy of law and its applications to practical situations.

Jurisprudence is published four times per year, to coincide with the four terms of the legal year, in an attractive paperback and electronic edition.

All authors who submit to this edition will be provided with a complementary copy of the journal.

Length: Any length is acceptable, although readability to non-specialist is key.

Presentation Style: Papers must comply with the Australian Guide to Legal Citations, Second Edition published by the Melbourne University Law Review. An electronic edition is available at, http://mulr.law.unimelb.edu.au/PDFs/aglc_dl.pdf

Submission: You must submit electronically in Microsoft Word format to editor@jurisprudence.com.au. Extraneous formatting is discouraged.

Correspondence can also be sent to this address. If you are considering submitting an article, you are invited to contact the editor to discuss ideas before authoring a work.

SUBSCRIPTION INFORMATION

The Journal is published four times per year in an attractive softcover book. Subscription to the Journal can be achieved by two methods:

1) Single issues can be purchased on amazon.com. Our publishers, the Elias Clark Group, set a retail price for each edition, typically AU$40. However, due to their agreement with amazon.com, the price may vary for retail customers.

2) A subscription to the Journal can be purchased for AU$150 per year, or AU$280 for two years. This price includes postage throughout the world. Payment can be made by international bank cheque, but not a personal cheque, to:

The Journal Jurisprudence,
C/o The Elias Clark Group
GPO Box 5001
Melbourne, Victoria, Australia.

Alternatively, the Journal is available online at www.jurisprudence.com.au and can be read there free of charge.

EDITORIAL: THE JURISPRUDENCE OF TORTS

Law students are often told that controversy only arises at the periphery of law. Most cases of murder, for example, are questions of fact, not law. Only when we consider extraordinary cases, like the separation of Siamese twins,[1] or doctor assisted suicide, do we consider more basic question on the construction of law. The same could be said about the law of torts. The law of wrongs has a varied and interesting heritage stretching back to Roman law, yet, the history of torts is not frequently cited in cases of negligence or duty of care. Yet, in assembling this issue, we have brought together eminent thinkers to engage with the question of torts, as a whole, not just in specific fact-based cases.

The young scholar Jonathan Blackmore of Shepard Broad Law Centre, Nova Southeastern University introduces us to the use of the writings of Franz Kafka in the American case law. Particularly, he engages with cases that use (and misuse) the term Kafkaesque. His insightful article gives us insight not into the *ratio* of modern case law, but the legal voice that has emerged from popular literature. It is with pleasure that we publish *The Influence of Franz Kafka on American Jurisprudence.*

Ms. Brooke Glass-O'Shea of the University of Southern California writes for us on cultural claims in American courts. From the 'thin skull' principle to various other (and sometimes absurd) civil claims, she enlightens us to how membership in a minority group has been grounds for additional damages in courts. Ms. Glass-O'Shea has produced an article worthy of our praise it is an honour to include *The Cultural Offense: How and Why Plaintiffs Bring Cultural Claims To Court* in this fourth edition of *Jurisprudence.*

Mr Joshua Masters of New York University is a truly innovative scholar, a growing leader in his field who writes on the topic of rational choice theory in law. Few lawyers find the opportunity to engage with macro questions and Mr Masters has skilfully and elegantly elucidated an original theory of rational choice in legal decision making. I have no doubt that this article will be of importance to generations to come.

Associate Professor Robert L. McFarland writes on the teaching of the law of wrongs in American law schools. Professor McFarland brings the insights of a dedicated legal educator, but also from a religious perspective, for he teaches at the Faulkner University. A Christian educator, just like his colleague Associate

[1] See, e.g., Re A (Children) (Conjoined Twins: Surgical Separation) [2000] 4 All ER 961.

Professor Adam McLeod who wrote in the first edition of *Jurisprudence*, Professor McFarland brings a genuine passion about legal education to his article *Teaching the Law of Wrongs without Searching for What is Right.* The depth of jurisprudential scholarship by Professors McFarland and MacLeod clearly positions Faulkner University among the bourgeoning centres of contemporary, passionate jurisprudential scholarship.

Finally, this is the fourth edition of *Jurisprudence* and, therefore, one year since our first publication. The journal has grown leaps and bound in this short time. Everyday, I wake up to an inbox filled with the most exciting legal scholarship from every corner of the globe. In the next issue, we will engage with question of religion and jurisprudence. For 2010, we have the honour of Dr.Jur. Eric Engle and Mr Richard Mullender to each guest edit an edition.

Aron Ping D'Souza
Editor

Oxford, 14 October 2009

THE CULTURAL OFFENSE: HOW AND WHY PLAINTIFFS BRING CULTURAL CLAIMS TO COURT

Ms. Brooke Glass-O'Shea[1]
The University of Southern California

I. Introduction

In her book, *The Cultural Defense*, Alison Dundes Renteln asserts that courts of law should be required to consider "cultural" evidence. Her argument is largely based on the idea that, because "culture shapes cognition and conduct," evidence about a person's culture is necessary to understand that person's motivations.[2] Defendants' motivations, Renteln argues, are directly relevant to the amount of blame, and therefore the amount of punishment, they deserve.[3]

Despite the book's title, Renteln includes a number of cases in which the culture in question is that of a civil plaintiff rather than a criminal defendant. That is, some of Renteln's cases are not about cultural defenses but instead cultural offenses. In these cases, it is plaintiffs who seek to introduce evidence of their own culture in order to explain why a defendant's act was offensive, or why the act may have caused the damage it did. How might such evidence be used, and in what kind of case?

One classic example is the case of Mukesh K. Rai, a Hindu man who sued Taco Bell after mistakenly being served a beef burrito.[4] Rai explained to the Los Angeles Times that "the cow is a sacred animal to Hindus, considered a mother to everyone."[5] Though Taco Bell settled with Rai, some members of the public were dubious of Rai's claims and offended by what they saw as "cultural sensitivity" gone haywire.[6]

---

[1] Brooke Glass-O'Shea received her JD from the University of Southern California, and is currently studying sustainable international development at the University of Washington School of Law. She would like to thank Professor Chris Stone, who provided ideas and support for this article, and Wayne State University Law School, who originally published an alternate version of this article in The Journal of Law in Society. Please send any questions or comments to bigo@u.washington.edu.

[2] Renteln, Alison Dundes. *The Cultural Defense*, p. 6. New York: Oxford University Press, 2004.

[3] *Id.* at 189.

[4] *Id.* at 107.

[5] MacGregor, Hilary. "Faith and Food." *Los Angeles Times*. Jan. 25, 1998, A3.

[6] For example, the Humanist Association of San Diego's newsletter described the case as a "church-state threat" and rhetorically demanded, "How could such a 'devout Hindu' expect to placidly eat even a bean burrito while, all around him, others were munching on his ancestors?" Such an argument may reflect Christian-derived ideas about belief and tolerance, as Hindus,

The public reaction to the Rai case reveals the tension that is inherent to issues of group rights. As a society, we value diversity, but we also believe that people should be treated equally. Does this mean that different people should be treated differently, or that different people should be treated as though they were the same? Some scholars, such as Thomas Pogge, have argued that membership in a particular group should never be a basis for differential treatment, both because group membership is often subjective and unclear and also because true equality demands equal treatment (at least in the public domain) of all citizens, "regardless of their identifications and affiliations."[7] In Pogge's view, granting special status to members of a particular group can only be justified in reference to the circumstances facing the individuals in the group, and therefore the special status must also be extended to anyone else who shares those circumstances.

Christopher Stone, in discussing Pogge's hypothesis, offers the example of Quakers being given exemptions from "hostile military service" by the United States.[8] Stone argues that such an exemption may be permissible if based on two premises: that every individual's core convictions should be respected equally, and that Quakers, by their affiliation with an anti-violence religious group, have "signaled" their core-level commitment to non-violence.[9] While I agree with Pogge and Stone in the abstract, such formulations may be difficult to apply in a legal context, where judges must navigate the messy, conflicting reality of actual human values. How could a non-Quaker prove to a judge his core belief in non-violence? Suppose a secular humanist sued the U.S. government for conscientious objector status, arguing that harming any human being offended his deeply-felt belief in the sanctity of human life. How might he prove this, and how much deference should his beliefs be given?[10]

Mukesh K. Rai might agree that everyone's core convictions should be respected equally, and might further argue that, in serving him a beef burrito, the employees of Taco Bell betrayed this principle. But even if the employees knew or should have known of Rai's beliefs (which seems unlikely,[11] but would have to be proven to make the action a tort), what would it mean to treat Rai's

---

unlike many Christians, do not believe that non-believers should be made to follow Hindu practices or proscriptions. <http://www.godless.org/hasd/hnl04.html>, accessed 9/29/07.

[7] Pogge, Thomas W. "Group Rights and Ethnicity," in *Ethnicity and Group Rights*, p. 188. Ian Shapiro and Will Kymlicka, eds. New York: New York University Press, 1997.
[8] Stone, Christopher. "Groups in Law and Morals: The Case of Aboriginal Subsistence Whaling." Draft of speech delivered at the University of Oslo.
[9] Id.
[10] According to one district court, "Whenever a belief system encompasses fundamental questions of the nature of reality and relationship of human beings to reality, it deals with essentially religious questions." *Alabama and Coushatta Tribes of Texas v. Trustees of the Big Sandy Ind. Sch. Dist.*, 817 F. Supp. 1319, 1329 (E.D. Tex. 1993), citing *Smith v. Board of School Com'rs of Mobile County*, 655 F. Supp. 939, 979 (S.D.Ala.), as holding "that secular humanism is a religious belief system entitled to the protections of the religion clause."
[11] See the *Yang* case, discussed in the Constitutional Claims section, *infra*, for an example of a court finding that a defendant knew or should have known of a plaintiff's religious beliefs.

beliefs "equally"? Equal, that is, to what? Should Rai's aversion to beef be treated like a Muslim's aversion to eating pork, or like an average American's aversion to eating dogs? Should it be given more weight than a lifelong vegetarian's aversion to beef? What if the vegetarian is also an ardent animal-rights activist, and Rai recently converted to Hinduism, or neglects numerous commandments of that faith?

These are hard questions, and I do not propose to answer them in this paper. Instead, I wish to show some of the many different ways that plaintiffs may use cultural claims in the courtroom, and in the process illuminate some of the difficulties inherent to weighing a plaintiff's beliefs against the rights and demands of other individuals, groups, and the state. I will discuss culture in the context of tort claims, hate speech, constitutional claims, witness credibility, and statutory law. I will then describe some of the ways in which testimony about cultural beliefs or practices should and should not be presented in court. In the last section, I will address the growing international movement to afford legal protection to elements of indigenous cultures.

Note on Religion and Culture

For this paper, I will not generally distinguish between religious and cultural claims, except where the law makes such a distinction. There are two reasons for this. First, religion is a part of culture, and usually inextricably entwined with it, so the religious claims I will discuss are always cultural claims as well. Second, due to recent developments in First Amendment jurisprudence, plaintiffs in the United States may need to characterize their claims as either religious exercise or cultural expression, or even both, depending on which law governs their particular situation. However, beliefs about morality, diet, the body, and many other things may be fairly characterized either way. By describing religious claims as cultural, I hope to erode the rather artificial distinction that allows us to privilege one over the other.

II. Tort Cases

A. The Cultural "Thin-Skull" Tort

On August 22, 1963, a 16-year-old girl named Ruth Friedman got on a ski lift with her friend, Jack.[12] The pair had enjoyed an afternoon of picnicking and "sightseeing" on the mountain, and were ready to return home for the day. As they rode down the mountain, the lift suddenly stopped, and the two teenagers were suspended, helplessly, 25 feet above the ground. They yelled for help, but no one came, and Ruth started to panic. She jumped from the lift and, despite numerous injuries, managed to get down the mountain and call the police.

In her case against the State of New York, which owned and operated the ski lift, Ruth Friedman argued that her ultra-orthodox Jewish upbringing and beliefs compelled her to jump in order to avoid spending the night alone with a man. Rabbi Herschel Stahl gave expert testimony that a Hebrew law known as the Jichud strictly forbids a man and woman to stay together in a private place. A woman who violated this law would destroy her own reputation and that of

[12] The facts of this case are from *Friedman v. State*, 54 Misc. 2d 448 (N.Y. 1967).

her parents. The court accepted the rabbi's testimony, and awarded damages to Friedman and her father.

The Friedman case is an excellent example of a cultural thin skull case. The term "thin skull" refers to a tort case in which the victim sustains "extra" damages due to a pre-existing condition.[13] Though the Restatement spells out this rule in terms of a pre-existing *physical* condition,[14] it also describes the rule as part of a "broader rule" allowing damages for harm which was unexpected and unforeseeable.[15] In other words, a tortfeasor "takes his victim as he finds him."[16]

The thin skull doctrine works well with cultural claims because it requires an *underlying* offense. That is, the doctrine only comes into play once a plaintiff has established that the defendant committed a tort, as measured by the usual "objective" standard of foreseeable harm.[17] It seems fair that, when someone is harmed by someone else's bad behavior, the cost of the harm should be borne by the guilty party rather than the innocent victim.

In the Friedman case, the court took pains to establish that the State had been negligent in its operation of the ski lift, citing no less than five different examples of negligence. These included failing to notify passengers of the hours of operation, failing to search one side of the mountain before leaving for the day, and failing to announce over the loudspeaker that the lift was closing. This negligence had nothing to do with Ruth Friedman's culture or religion. The State was negligent because it knew or should have known that its behavior might cause a passenger to become stranded on the lift for the night, an experience that would surely be traumatic (and possibly hypothermia-inducing) for anyone from any cultural background.

---

13 See, e.g., *Lee v. Regan*, 47 N.C. App. 544, 550 (N.C. Ct. App. 1980) (applying the "special sensitivity" or "thin skull" rule in an auto collision case where plaintiff's preexisting spinal cord disease was aggravated by the crash); *Vosburg v. Putney*, 80 Wis. 523 (Wis. 1891) (landmark case allowing recovery where one schoolboy lightly kicked another on the shin, thereby reopening a recently healed wound).

14 "The negligent actor is subject to liability for harm to another although a physical condition of the other which is neither known nor should be known to the actor makes the injury greater than that which the actor as a reasonable man should have foreseen as a probable result of his conduct." Restat. 2d of Torts, § 461.

15 Id., Comment (b).

16 *Bryan v. City of New Orleans*, 737 So. 2d 696, 698 (La. 1999) (allowing recovery where a police officer treated plaintiff roughly, exacerbating his already fragile emotional state and causing him to require psychiatric care).

17 Note the Restatement's reference to the "negligent actor"; see also *Bryan*, 737 So. 2d at 698 (a defendant "is responsible for all the natural and probable consequences of his *tortious* conduct" [emphasis added]).

What role, then, did Friedman's beliefs and the rabbi's testimony play in the case? The State had moved to dismiss the case on two grounds: that its own negligence had not been proven, and that Friedman was *contributorily negligent.* Though the court did not mention any of Friedman's personal characteristics in its finding of negligence by the State, it did refer to Friedman's "age, judgment, experience, and education" in support of its finding that she was not contributorily negligent.[18] Near the beginning of the opinion, the court made the explicit finding that Friedman became hysterical while trapped on the lift, citing both the normal distress that "a lightly dressed 16 year old city girl" would feel in such a situation *and* the extra distress Friedman must have felt because of the "moral compulsion" she believed herself to be under.[19] Because Friedman could not control either of these factors, she was not contributorily negligent when she jumped off of the ski lift.

This treatment of Friedman's cultural evidence is very analogous to the treatment of medical evidence in a thin skull tort case. In both situations, the court must find that the defendant's conduct was tortious (whether intentional, reckless, or negligent), an analysis that does not involve the plaintiff's pre-existing condition (medical or cultural) because such condition "is neither known nor should be known" by the defendant.[20] If the defendant acted tortiously, then he is responsible for *all* of the damage caused by his act. The plaintiff cannot be held responsible (or, legally speaking, contributorily negligent) for a pre-existing condition beyond her control, even if it exacerbates the damage. The rabbi's testimony was like that of a doctor, who in a regular thin skull tort case would testify about the nature of the plaintiff's condition and how it might have contributed to the plaintiff's damages.

Friedman's jump from the ski lift may have been an unusual reaction to the situation, perhaps even so unusual as to be unforeseeable. But if Friedman had suffered from an "unforeseeable" medical condition like severe diabetes, she might have jumped off the lift to avoid going into insulin shock and possibly falling. In that situation, the State of New York would be liable for all damages under the traditional thin skull rule. This seems fair, because the State was negligent, while Friedman would not be held at fault for having diabetes. If we agree with the judge that Friedman was not at fault for holding ultra-orthodox religious beliefs, then it makes sense that the cost of her resulting damages is more fairly borne by the negligent State than by the innocent Friedman family.

B. Culture Used to Assess Damages

---

[18] *Friedman*, 54 Misc. 2d at 456.

[19] *Id.* at 452.

[20] Restat. 2d of Torts, § 461.

In addition to explaining a plaintiff's behavior, cultural evidence may also be used to illuminate the plaintiff's relationships with other people. In the damages context, such evidence can help a jury to measure the plaintiff's loss when a loved one is hurt or killed in an accident. This was the case in *In Re Air Crash Disaster Near New Orleans*,[21] a consolidation of the claims of three Uruguayan citizens arising out of the 1982 crash of Pan American Flight 759.

Ernesto Serio Pampin-Lopez was one of the plaintiffs in *New Orleans*. Pampin lost his mother, sister, and an aunt in the crash, and sought damages for the loss of his mother's and sister's love and affection. The jury awarded him fairly large sums for these nonpecuniary losses: $250,000 for his mother and $150,000 for his sister. The Court of Appeals reduced the award for Pampin's sister because it could not find any comparable award for a sibling's love and affection in the case law, but it upheld the award for Pampin's mother. In doing so, the court cited evidence of the unusual closeness of the Pampin family:

> There were daily contacts encompassing every facet of their lives. When Pampin married, rather than draw away from his consanguineal family, he brought his wife into that close unit. They worked, lived, and played together. Pampin looked to his principled and strong-charactered mother for guidance and advice in personal and business matters.[22]

Though the *New Orleans* case was eventually separated into two trials, both juries were put together initially to hear the testimony of three witnesses. Two of these were women who witnessed the plane crash. The third was a Tulane University anthropologist, who gave testimony "about South American mores and familial relations."[23] Though the appeals court did not mention how the anthropologist's testimony was used, it seems clear that it was deemed both relevant and important to the Uruguayan plaintiffs' claims, and that it provided support for the more specific evidence about the closeness of the Pampin family.

An anthropologist provided similar evidence in another airplane crash case, *Saavedra v. Korean Air Lines*,[24] which arose after Korean Air Lines Flight KE007 was shot down over the Sea of Japan by Soviet missiles in 1983. The plaintiff in *Saavedra* represented the estate of a married Japanese couple, Makoto and Yoko Okai, both of whom died in the crash, and also brought claims on behalf of the Okais' parents for loss of support. In upholding the jury's award on these claims, the Court of Appeals cited the testimony of a cultural anthropologist, who explained "that in Japanese culture, the Okais' parents could reasonably

21 789 F.2d 1092 (5th Cir. 1986).
22 *Id.* at 1099-1100.
23 *Id.* at 1095.
24 93 F.3d 547 (9th Cir. 1996).

expect support from the Okais."[25] This doubtlessly added weight to the testimony given by the Okais' parents that they had expected their adult children to help support them as they got older.

III. Group Libel and Hate Speech

Members of minority races, religions, and cultures may be subjected to hurtful words aimed at their identities – what is now popularly known as "hate speech." What legal recourse, if any, do members of stigmatized groups have in this situation?

In the 1952 case of *Beauharnais v. Illinois*, the Supreme Court upheld an Illinois law that criminalized the "publication or exhibition" of materials written against a particular race or religion.[26] This was not a cultural offense case, but rather a criminal defendant's free speech challenge to the Illinois law, which he was convicted under after distributing racist leaflets in Chicago.[27] However, the Illinois Supreme Court characterized the law as "a form of criminal libel law," and it was treated that way by the courts.[28] Thus, the Court's ruling left the gate open for potential libel actions by members of racial or cultural minorities victimized by hate speech.

However, by the 1970s, the courts had narrowed *Beauharnais* into virtual nonexistence.[29] For example, in 1978, the Seventh Circuit Court of Appeals struck down a local ordinance in Skokie, Illinois, with language remarkably similar to the statute in *Beauharnais*.[30] The court held that the Supreme Court "rewrote the rules" with the intervening free speech and libel cases, so that libel had become subject to First Amendment considerations.[31] Though *Beauharnais* had not been explicitly overruled (and still has not been), the court found that,

---

[25] *Id.* at 554.

[26] 343 U.S. 250 (1952). The relevant statute read: "It shall be unlawful for any person, firm or corporation to manufacture, sell, or offer for sale, advertise or publish, present or exhibit in any public place in this state any lithograph, moving picture, play, drama or sketch, which publication or exhibition portrays depravity, criminality, unchastity, or lack of virtue of a class of citizens, of any race, color, creed or religion which said publication or exhibition exposes the citizens of any race, color, creed or religion to contempt, derision, or obloquy or which is productive of breach of the peace or riots. . . ."

[27] *Id.* at 252.

[28] *Id.* at 253-54.

[29] See, e.g., *Tollett v. United States*, 485 F.2d 1087, 1094 (8th Cir. 1973) (finding that "it is extremely doubtful that the Illinois statute then existing [in *Beauharnais*] would be upheld today"); *Collin v. Smith*, 578 F.2d 1197 (7th Cir. 1978); *American Booksellers Assoc. v. Hudnut*, 771 F.2d 323, 332 (7th Cir. 1985) (citing *Collin* as holding that recent Supreme Court free speech cases "had so washed away the foundations of *Beauharnais* that it could not be considered authoritative").

[30] *Collin v. Smith*, 578 F.2d 1197 (7th Cir. 1978).

[31] *Id.* at 1205.

if *Beauharnais* was good law at all, it stood for the proposition that extremely prejudicial speech could be banned if it was likely to incite violence.[32] This situation may have applied to mid-century Illinois, which had been "the scene of exacerbated tension between races, often flaring into violence and destruction,"[33] but it seems less likely to be invoked today.

Though the above cases involve criminal libel, the free speech consideration given to libelous speech applies in civil cases as well. Thus, potential damage to an individual's reputation must be balanced against the general presumption in favor of free speech. For this reason, tort suits for "group libel" are not generally allowed unless a plaintiff can show that the allegedly defamatory statements refer to him specifically, and not just to a group to which he belongs.[34] This may be the case if the group referred to is sufficiently small – generally, less than 25 people[35] -- or if the statements are made in such a way that the plaintiff is implicitly referred to. These requirements effectively preclude suits for "cultural" hate speech, unless the statement is a thinly veiled reference to a specific individual.[36]

One example of a cultural libel claim is the case of *Anyanwu v. Columbia Broadcasting System.*[37] In *Anyanwu*, a Nigerian man sued CBS, Ed Bradley, Andy Rooney, and Mike Wallace after an episode of CBS's "60 Minutes" accused Nigerian businessmen of defrauding Americans. The plaintiff, Tony Anyanwu, claimed to represent the entire class of Nigerians doing business with United States citizens, but the district court held that Anyanwu could not bring a claim because the alleged defamatory statements did not refer to him particularly, and the group he claimed to represent was too large (over 500 individuals). "It is not sufficient," wrote the court, "that the plaintiff is libeled as a member of a large group."[38]

---

32 *Id.* at 1204.

33 *Beauharnais*, 343 U.S. at 259.

34 Restat. 2d of Torts, § 564A.

35 Id. at Illustration 2b; see also, e.g., *Gintert v. Howard Publications*, 565 F. Supp. 829 (D. Ind. 1983) (no group libel claim allowed for plaintiff class of approximately 165 property owners); *Arcand v. Evening Call Pub. Co.*, 567 F.2d 1163 (1st Cir. 1977) (no group libel claim for statement about one unidentified member of a 21-person group); *Weatherhead v. Globe International, Inc.*, 832 F.2d 1226 (10th Cir. 1987) (affirming that a "claimant group of 955 was too large to afford relief" for group libel).

36 For example, the statement that "Amish people eat babies" may be actionable if directed at the only Amish family in town (especially if there is a baby missing).

37 887 F. Supp. 690 (D.N.Y. 1995).

38 887 F. Supp. at 692, *citing Church of Scientology Int'l v. Time Warner*, 806 F. Supp. 1157, 1160 (D.N.Y. 1992).

Though not usually actionable in a civil case, hate speech may still be prohibited by law because it may be narrowly defined so as to fit within the "fighting words" exception to the First Amendment protection of speech.[39] However, as the Supreme Court held in *R. A. V. v. St. Paul*, such a prohibition would have to apply equally to all groups in order to avoid unconstitutional content or viewpoint discrimination.[40] In *R.A.V.*, the Court struck down a St. Paul, Minnesota, ordinance that criminalized hate speech directed at a person's "race, color, creed, religion or gender," noting that the law did not cover, for example, "political affiliation, union membership, or homosexuality."[41] Justice Scalia's reasoning for the majority was strikingly similar to Pogge's argument, discussed in the Introduction above, that equal protection should never be contingent upon membership in any particular group or type of group.

It is important here to note the distinction between "hate speech" and "hate crimes." The two may seem to contain similar elements – i.e., the official punishment of biased or hate-motivated beliefs. However, hate speech is generally protected by the First Amendment and, under *R. A. V.*, may only be regulated by narrowly-drawn, content-neutral laws. In contrast, the bias element that turns a crime into a "hate crime" is not considered to be "speech" for First Amendment purposes.[42] As the Supreme Court explained in *Wisconsin v. Mitchell*, such bias is simply a motive for the crime, and may be taken into consideration for sentencing purposes like any other motive.[43]

IV. Constitutional Claims

A. Free Exercise of Religion

You Vang Yang and Ia Kue Yang came to the United States from Laos.[44] They were Hmong, a minority ethnic group found in southern China and Southeast Asia, with their own customs, language, and religious beliefs. On December 21, 1987, their 23-year-old son, Neng Yang, had a seizure and lost consciousness. He was taken to Rhode Island Hospital, and died there three days later without ever regaining consciousness. The doctors at the hospital could not explain what caused the young man's seizure or death.

An assistant resident at the hospital contacted the Rhode Island Medical Examiners' Office to report the unexplained death. The Assistant Medical

---

39 See *Chaplinsky v. New Hampshire,* 315 U.S. 568 (1942).

40 505 U.S. 377, 391-92 (1992).

41 *Id.* at 391.

42 *Wisconsin v. Mitchell*, 508 U.S. 476, 487 (1993) (holding that a Wisconsin statute providing penalty enhancements for bias-motivated crimes was "aimed at conduct unprotected by the First Amendment").

43 *Id.* at 485.

44 The facts of this case are from *Yang v. Sturner*, 728 F. Supp. 845 (R.I. 1990).

Examiner had Neng Yang's body sent over. The next day, Dr. William Sturner, the Chief Medical Examiner for the State of Rhode Island, performed an autopsy on the body but could not determine a cause of death.

The Hmong believe that human bodies must never be mutilated, even after death. Neng Yang's parents would never have consented to the autopsy, but Dr. Sturner did not consult them. Instead, he relied on state law, which permits autopsies where there is a reasonable suspicion that the death was caused by (among other things) a criminal act or "an infectious agent capable of spreading an epidemic within the state."[45] The doctor decided that it was necessary to perform an autopsy on Neng Yang in order to "ensure that the cause of death was not attributable to some act or agent that posed a threat to the health, safety and welfare of the citizens of . . . Rhode Island."[46]

The Yangs were devastated. They believed that, because of the autopsy, "the spirit of Neng would not be free, therefore his spirit will come back and take another person in his family."[47] They sued Dr. Sturner, both individually and in his official capacity, for violating their rights to religious freedom, due process, and equal protection, as well as various state law claims. The district court held that, while the Yangs could not sue for damages under 42 U.S.C. § 1983, they had a valid *Bivens* claim for the violation of their First Amendment rights.[48]

In analyzing the Yangs' First Amendment claims, the court primarily cited to *Wisconsin v. Yoder*[49] and *Sherbert v. Verner*,[50] two cases in which the Supreme Court applied strict scrutiny to laws that burdened the free exercise of religion. The district court found that the Yangs' beliefs had been violated to an even greater extent than the parties in *Yoder* and *Sherbert*. Moreover, the court found no "compelling state interest" which could justify such a violation. Also, Dr. Sturner was not entitled to qualified immunity as a government official, because a reasonable medical examiner would have known that some citizens of Rhode Island, including the Hmong, have profound religious objections to autopsies. Therefore, Dr. Sturner should have known that performing an autopsy on a

---

45 *Id.* at 847.

46 Id.

47 *Yang v. Sturner*, 750 F. Supp. 558, 558 (R.I. 1990b).

48 In *Bivens v. Six Unknown Named Agents of the FBI*, 403 U.S. 388 (1971), the Supreme Court held that a private right of action for damages may be implied for violation of a plaintiff's constitutional rights where there is no other federal remedy available.

49 406 U.S. 205 (1972). In *Yoder*, the Supreme Court held that the Amish must be given an exception to the Wisconsin law requiring children to stay in school until the age of 16. The Amish feared that keeping their children in school beyond the 8th grade would expose them to "worldly" and unhealthy influences.

50 374 U.S. 398 (1963). In *Sherbert*, the Supreme Court held that a state could not deny unemployment benefits to someone who was fired for refusing to work on the Sabbath.

body that might be Hmong "would violate the religious beliefs of the decedent's next of kin."[51] The court found that Dr. Sturner was liable to the Yangs for the emotional distress he had caused them, and ordered a future hearing to be scheduled on the extent of damages.

Unfortunately for the Yangs, their victory was short-lived. Several months after the district court's initial opinion, the U.S. Supreme Court decided the case of *Employment Division, Department of Human Resources of Oregon v. Smith*,[52] which essentially overturned the compelling interest test for free exercise, as used in *Yoder* and *Sherbert*. The district court judge, after reading the *Smith* decision, issued an addendum withdrawing his original opinion and dismissing the case with prejudice.

What went wrong? It wasn't the Yangs' cultural evidence. Dr. Sturner had not even attempted to challenge the Yangs' stated beliefs or the centrality of those beliefs to the Hmong religion. And the judge was profoundly moved by their plight, stating:

"I have seldom, in twenty-four years on the bench, seen such a sincere instance of emotion displayed. I could not help but also notice the reaction of the large number of Hmongs who had gathered to witness the hearing. Their silent tears shed in the still courtroom as they heard the Yangs' testimony provided stark support for the depth of the Yangs' grief."[53]

The problem was that, after *Smith*, "state laws of general applicability" are not subject to restriction by the free exercise clause.[54] That is, governmental laws or actions may violate people's religious beliefs with impunity, so long as they are not targeting a particular group. For the Yangs, this meant that it did not matter if their religious freedom was burdened, because Dr. Sturner had acted in accordance with a neutral, generally applicable state law governing autopsies. The judge for the Yangs made it perfectly clear that he did not agree with this result, nor with the *Smith* majority's reading of the relevant legal precedent, but that he was "constrained to apply the majority's opinion to the instant case."[55]

The *Smith* decision marked the end of the U.S. Supreme Court's overhaul of free exercise jurisprudence that, arguably, began with *Bowen v. Roy*[56] in 1986. The plaintiff in *Roy* was a Native American man who refused to obtain a Social Security number for his 2-year-old daughter, Little Bird of the Snow. He believed that the number would rob his daughter's spirit and keep her from

[51] 728 F. Supp. at 855.
[52] 494 U.S. 872 (1990).
[53] 750 F. Supp. at 558.
[54] *Smith*, 494 U.S. at 908 (Blackmun, J. dissenting).
[55] 750 F. Supp. at 559.
[56] 476 U.S. 693 (1986).

attaining spiritual purity and power. Because Roy would not provide a Social Security number for his daughter, the Pennsylvania Department of Public Welfare terminated the girl's benefits, medical insurance, and food stamps. The Supreme Court found that Roy's religious freedom was not violated by government use of a Social Security number. "The Free exercise Clause," held the Court, "simply cannot be understood to require the Government to conduct its own internal affairs in ways that comport with the religious beliefs of particular citizens."[57] The Court emphasized that Roy's freedom to express and exercise his religion had not been impaired.

Two years later, the Court expanded on *Roy* in the case of *Lyng v. Northwest Indian Cemetery Protective Association.*[58] In the *Lyng* case, the U.S. Forest Service sought to build a road and harvest timber in a part of the Six Rivers National Forest traditionally used by local American Indians for religious rituals. The Forest Service's own study concluded that the area was an indispensable part of the Indians' religion and that the planned road would seriously damage the Indian sacred area, but the Forest Service decided to go ahead with their plan anyway. The Indians, along with some nature groups and the State of California, filed suit to enjoin the road and the timber harvesting. The district court issued the injunction, finding that the road and the timber harvesting would violate the Indians' free exercise rights.[59]

The Supreme Court, however, did not agree. In fact, the majority found that the Forest Service's plan "cannot meaningfully be distinguished from the use of a Social Security number in *Roy*."[60] Strangely enough, these words were written by Justice O'Connor, who had written a partial dissent in *Roy*. There, O'Connor argued that the government did not need to compel Roy to provide his daughter's Social Security number, and that such compulsion was a religious burden that could only be justified by "an especially important governmental interest pursued by narrowly tailored means."[61] In *Lyng*, however, O'Connor wrote that the two cases were comparable in that neither the Indian plaintiffs *nor* the plaintiffs in *Roy* would be "coerced by the Government's action into violating their religious beliefs."[62] Even if the Forest Service plan would "virtually destroy the . . . Indians' ability to practice their religion,"[63] this was

57 476 U.S. at 699.

58 485 U.S. 439 (1988).

59 Northwest Indian Cemetery Protective Ass'n v. Peterson, 565 F. Supp. 586 (D. Cal. 1983).

60 485 U.S. at 449.

61 476 U.S. at 728. O'Connor was applying the *Sherbert* test to Roy's religious burden.

62 485 U.S. at 449.

63 Id. at 451, quoting Northwest Indian Cemetery Protective Ass'n v. Peterson, 795 F.2d 688, 693 (9th Cir. 1986).

not a burden on the free exercise of religion because the Indians were not being coerced into doing anything.

Justices Brennan and Marshall, both of whom had joined O'Connor's dissent in *Roy*, dissented from her opinion in *Lyng*, along with Justice Blackmun. The Free Exercise Clause, wrote Brennan, covers more than just coercion or penalizing religious behavior; it covers any government action that frustrates the practice of religion. The majority had achieved its perfect analogy to *Roy* only by ignoring that decision's emphasis on internal government affairs and the lack of impairment to Roy's ability to practice his religion.

After *Lyng*, the stage was set for *Smith*. In that case, two members of the Native American Church lost their jobs because they ingested peyote in a church ceremony, and were subsequently denied unemployment compensation. The Supreme Court was not sympathetic. Religious belief, wrote Scalia for the majority, cannot excuse anyone from following a neutral, generally applicable law. All of the Court's previous cases that appeared to hold otherwise were actually based on free exercise claims *plus* some other constitutional claim, like freedom of speech (though the cases themselves did not make this distinction). Free exercise claims alone did not merit strict scrutiny, or any scrutiny at all, unless the government was targeting a particular religion on purpose. After all, Scalia reasoned, why should the government have to adjust its drug laws to account for religious practice when it did not have to adjust its land management, as per *Lyng*, or its administration of public benefits, as per *Roy*?

Again, Brennan, Marshall, and Blackmun dissented. Even O'Connor shied away from Scalia's abandonment of religious strict scrutiny. She concurred in the judgment, but only because she found enforcing drug laws to be a compelling state interest sufficient to overcome the obvious burden on the peyote users' religious practice.

While the *Smith* decision was a fatal blow to the *Yang* case, it was certainly not the last word on the issue. In 1993, Congress passed the Religious Freedom Restoration Act ("RFRA"), whose express purpose was to overturn *Smith* and "restore the compelling interest test as set forth in *Sherbert v. Verner* . . . and *Wisconsin v. Yoder*."[64] Four years later, the Supreme Court struck down the RFRA, at least as applied to state law, in *City of Boerne v. Flores*.[65] While acknowledging Congress's authority to enforce First Amendment guarantees through legislation, the Court held that Congress did not have the authority "to decree the substance of the Amendment's restrictions on the State. [. . .]

[64] 42 USCS § 2000bb et seq.
[65] 521 U.S. 507, 529-36 (1997).

Congress does not enforce a constitutional right by changing what the right is."[66]

It appears, then, that if a case similar to *Yang* were brought today, it would probably fail (at least in Rhode Island). This scenario was played out in *Kickapoo Traditional Tribe of Texas v. Chacon*,[67] a 1999 Texas case reminiscent of *Yang*. In *Kickapoo*, a Native woman named Norma Rodriguez died of apparent asphyxiation. Martha Chacon, the local Justice of the Peace, ordered an autopsy, allegedly with the approval of Rodriguez's mother. Various tribal members and County officials tried to dissuade Chacon, arguing that Rodriguez had been an inhalant abuser and had clearly died from inhaling paint fumes. In the meantime, Rodriguez was buried on tribal land. When Chacon learned of this, she ordered the body disinterred so that an autopsy could be performed. This was unacceptable to the Kickapoo, who believe that "the scarring to the body caused by an autopsy and the disruption of a grave damages the spirit and can have adverse effect [sic] on the decedent's family."[68] The tribe filed suit and obtained a temporary restraining order against the disinterment. The State (as co-defendant) removed the case to district court.

The district court briefly discussed *Smith*, the RFRA, and *Boerne*, and concluded that the tribe's free exercise claim should be evaluated by the standard set in *Smith*. That is, a state law that burdens only free exercise of religion need not be justified by a compelling state interest, so long as the law is facially neutral and generally applicable. Such was the case with the Texas law allowing a justice of the peace to order an autopsy, so there was no First Amendment violation. The court noted that similar cases that went the other way were all decided before *Smith*, and cited to the *Yang* addendum for the proposition that an autopsy statute is facially neutral. The court vacated the restraining order and granted judgment for the defendants on all claims.

So did *Smith* mark the death of the free exercise clause? Not exactly. For one thing, Congress responded to the Supreme Court's decision in *Boerne* by enacting the Religious Land Use and Institutionalized Persons Act ("RLUIPA"),[69] a more carefully limited version of the RFRA. The RLUIPA applies to persons in federal or federally-funded institutions, which includes possibly the largest group of free exercise plaintiffs: prison inmates.

---

66 *Id.*

67 46 F. Supp. 2d 644 (W.D. Tex. 1999).

68 *Id.* at 651.

69 42 U.S.C. § 2000cc et seq. The RLUIPA was upheld by the Supreme Court in *Cutter v. Wilkinson*, 544 U.S. 709 (2005).

Under the RLUIPA, prison inmates enjoy a pre-*Smith* level of religious protection. This is demonstrated in the recent case of *Spratt v. Rhode Island Dept. of Corrections*,[70] in which Wesley Spratt, a convicted murderer and maximum-security prisoner, sued for the right to preach to other inmates. Spratt initially brought his claims under the RFRA, but since the RFRA did not apply after *Boerne* and the defendants acknowledged that Spratt could re-file his claims under the RLUIPA if necessary, the court and the parties decided to treat the complaint as filed under RLUIPA. The RLUIPA basically uses the old *Sherbert* test, in which a substantial burden on religious exercise can only be justified if there is (1) "a compelling government interest," and (2) the burdensome regulation "is the least restrictive means of furthering that compelling governmental interest."[71] Using this test, the district court found that Spratt's religious exercise was burdened by the prison's ban on inmate preaching, but that the ban was justified by the compelling need for prison security, which could not be accomplished by less restrictive means.

The Court of Appeals, however, was not convinced. The court noted that, because of Spratt's prima facie showing that his religious exercise had been substantially burdened, the burden of proof was shifted to the defendants to show that the preaching ban furthered a compelling state interest in the least restrictive fashion. While agreeing that prison security was indeed a compelling state interest, the court found that the defendants had not established that keeping Spratt from preaching was necessary for prison security. The defendants offered only one piece of evidence in support of their claim: an affidavit from the Assistant Director of Operations for the Rhode Island Department of Corrections, who stated that a prisoner who was allowed to preach would be perceived as a leader, and could abuse that power. The court, noting that the affidavit "cites no studies and discusses no research in support of its position,"[72] found the defendants' evidence insufficient. The defendants' other argument was that allowing prisoners to proselytize could lead to terrorist activity, as with some radical Muslim prisoners. This argument, said the court, only served to show that the prison had not given any individualized consideration to Spratt's case, as required by *Gonzales v. O Centro Espirita Beneficente Uniao do Vegetal*.[73] Spratt was an ordained Christian minister who had been preaching during weekly services for seven years – a far cry from a Muslim extremist.

Aside from RLUIPA, the other reason that free exercise is not dead is that religious practitioners still have some protection under *Smith*, if only against

---

70 482 F.3d 33 (1st Cir. 2007).

71 *Id.* at 37-38, quoting 42 U.S.C. § 2000cc-1(a).

72 *Id.* at 39.

73 546 U.S. 418 (2006).

overt discrimination. The Supreme Court made this point soon after *Smith* in *Church of the Lukumi Babalu Aye, Inc. v. City of Hialeah*,[74] the famous Florida Santeria case. Santeria, a syncretic Caribbean religion combining Catholic and animist elements, uses animal sacrifice as part of its rituals. The plaintiff in *Babalu Aye*, a Santeria church, planned to open a new house of worship, school, and cultural center in Hialeah, a town in South Florida. Many Hialeah residents were alarmed at this prospect. In response to citizens' concerns, the Hialeah city council passed several ordinances prohibiting ritual animal sacrifice. The ordinances carefully distinguished between the killing of animals for strictly food purposes and animal sacrifice, defined as "to unnecessarily kill, torment, torture, or mutilate an animal in a public or private ritual or ceremony not for the primary purpose of food consumption."[75] This distinction was necessary because Santeria practitioners usually eat the sacrificial animals after the rituals.

In the resulting lawsuit, the district court ruled for the defendant City, holding that any incidental burden on the plaintiffs' religious practice was fully justified by compelling governmental interests.[76] These included protecting public health from unsanitary animal remains, protecting children from the trauma of witnessing the sacrifices, protecting animals from inhumane treatment, and keeping animal slaughter within areas zoned for that purpose. The court made no factual findings to accompany its holding. The Court of Appeals affirmed, briefly noting that *Smith*, which came after the district court's decision, would have imposed an even more lenient standard on the City's restrictive regulations.

The Supreme Court, however, found that the City's regulations were invalid under *Smith*. The Court noted that the free exercise clause prohibits discrimination against religious beliefs or conduct. Though the city ordinances did not refer to a particular religion, their history, text (including references to "sacrifice" and "ritual"), and operation clearly revealed their intent to prohibit Santeria's practices. For example, while one ordinance prohibited the unnecessary killing of animals, this was interpreted by the City and the state Attorney General to include ritual killing but not hunting, fishing, euthanasia, killing animals for food, or even "the use of live rabbits to train greyhounds."[77] The Court could find no non-discriminatory justification for this preference for secular over religious reasons for killing animals, and therefore held that the ordinances were not neutral. Additionally, the City's alleged attempt to prevent animal cruelty and unsanitary waste disposal was addressed solely to religious

74 508 U.S. 520 (1993).

75 *Id.* at 527.

76 723 F. Supp. 1467 (SD Fla. 1989). This case came right before the Supreme Court decided *Smith*. The district court used the *Sherbert* balancing test.

77 *Id.* at 537, citing *Kiper v. State*, 310 So. 2d 42 (Fla. App. 1975).

sacrifice and not to other sources of those problems. Thus, the ordinances were not generally applicable either.

Because the ordinances were not neutral or generally applicable, the Court evaluated them with the highest level of scrutiny. Even if the state interests proffered by the City were compelling, the Court held, the ordinances were clearly not narrowly tailored to further those interests, for the same reasons that made them non-neutral and not generally applicable. The City's regulations therefore violated the church's First Amendment rights, and were invalid.

B. Other Constitutional Claims

In 1963, a high school teacher in Pasadena, California, was reassigned because he had grown a beard. He sued the school board.[78] The California Court of Appeal held that wearing a beard was a fundamental liberty interest protected by the Fourteenth Amendment's due process clause. Furthermore, the court found "that the wearing of a beard is a form of expression of an individual's personality," and therefore entitled to "peripheral" First Amendment protection.[79]

This case was cited by a Florida district court six years later, when another high school teacher was dismissed for refusing to shave off his goatee.[80] The Florida court found that the teacher, Booker C. Peek, should get at least as much protection for his goatee as the California plaintiff got for his beard. Additionally, the court bolstered its finding of First Amendment protection by quoting the plaintiff's assertion that the goatee was "an appropriate expression of his heritage, culture and racial pride as a black man."[81] Not only did the court accept the idea that a goatee might be a legitimate form of expression, it seemed to view the goatee-based discrimination as a proxy for racial discrimination. Even though there was no direct evidence of racial animus on the part of the school's Principal, the court found that his act of requesting that the plaintiff shave his goatee was "racially motivated . . . as a matter of law and fact." This was obvious, said the court, from the fact that Peek's dismissal bespoke an institutional "intolerance of ethnic diversity and racial pride."[82]

On the other side of the "right to hair" debate is the case of *New Rider v. Board of Education.*[83] The plaintiffs in *New Rider* were three Pawnee Indian children

---

[78] Finot v. Pasadena City Board of Education, 250 Cal. App. 2d 189 (1967).

[79] *Id.* at 199.

[80] The facts of this case are from *Braxton v. Board of Public Instruction*, 303 F. Supp. 958 (D. Fla. 1969).

[81] *Id.* at 959.

[82] *Id.* at 960. The court uses some fairly circular logic here – essentially, the Principal's discriminatory intent is proven by the discriminatory effect of his actions.

[83] 480 F.2d 693 (10th Cir. 1973).

who were suspended from school for having long hair. The dress code at their school dictated that students' hair must not be long enough to touch their ears or shirt collar. The children wanted long, braided hair because they saw it as a marker of pride in their Pawnee heritage and traditions. (It is perhaps ironic that the plaintiffs attended Pawnee Junior High School, in Pawnee County, Oklahoma.) An anthropologist named Dr. Weltfish testified that "such long braided hair has racial and cultural significance to the Pawnees" as well as religious significance, though she also testified that everything a Pawnee person does has religious significance.[84] Two other witnesses, presumably Pawnees, testified that young Indians were beginning to wear their hair long as part of a renewed interest in their traditions and culture. On the other hand, Dr. Muriel Wright, Editor of the Oklahoma Historical Society and author of a book on Oklahoma's Indian tribes, testified that the Pawnees did *not* have a tradition or custom of wearing long, braided hair.

The district court issued a preliminary injunction against the school board, finding that the plaintiffs' hairstyle was an expression of Pawnee heritage and religious identity. But one month later, the court reversed its findings and dismissed the complaint. The 10th Circuit Court of Appeals affirmed the dismissal, holding that the Pawnees' long hair was not a form of speech protected by the First Amendment. It was, rather, "speech-related conduct," which could be regulated under *U.S. v. O'Brian*[85] as long as the regulation served an important governmental interest and was narrowly tailored to that interest. The court accepted the school board's assertion that the hair regulation was necessary in order to maintain school spirit, unity, and discipline.

The Supreme Court declined to hear the *New Rider* case.[86] However, Justices Douglas and Marshall dissented from the denial of certiorari. Douglas protested the Court's persistent refusal to rule on the constitutionality of hair-length restrictions in schools, and noted that the Circuits were deeply divided on the issue. He was not impressed with the *New Rider* defendants' attempts to impose uniformity on students, especially in light of the historic discrimination against Indian pupils in American public schools. The Pawnee children's long hair, said Douglas, was intended to convey a specific message about their cultural pride.

---

[84] *Id.* at 696.

[85] 391 U.S. 367 (1968). In *U.S. v. O'Brian*, the Supreme Court upheld a law against destroying or mutilating draft cards. Such "speech-related conduct," held the Court, does not merit the same level of scrutiny as pure speech.

[86] New Rider v. Board of Education, 414 U.S. 1097 (1973).

As such, it merited the same level of First Amendment protection given to the plaintiff students in *Tinker v. Des Moines Indep. Cmty. School District.*[87]

These hair-related decisions reveal a profound uncertainty in the law about the importance of religious and cultural beliefs. Before *Smith*, a plaintiff was likely to bring a claim for the right to wear long hair under the free exercise clause. For example, in 1975, an incarcerated Native American man, Jerry Teterud, challenged a prison regulation that prevented him from wearing long, braided hair.[88] Teterud claimed that long hair was a part of his religion, and presented testimony from two anthropologists and a Native American spiritual leader to support his contention. The district court found that the hair regulation as applied to Teterud was unconstitutional, and the Court of Appeals affirmed, noting that the prison's interests in cleanliness and security could be satisfied by less restrictive means. Similar cases include *Moskowitz v. Wilkinson*,[89] in which an Orthodox Jewish inmate won the right to wear a beard in prison, and *Kahane v. Carlson*,[90] in which another Jewish inmate won the right to be given kosher food.

Today, such inmate claims would probably be brought under the RLUIPA, which still offers substantial free exercise protection. (If Mukesh K. Rai had been served a beef burrito in prison instead of at a Taco Bell, perhaps he would have had a stronger claim.) But for plaintiffs who aren't in prison, free exercise claims can be difficult to negotiate after *Smith*. In the case of *Alabama and Coushatta Tribes of Texas v. Trustees of the Big Sandy Ind. Sch. Dist.*,[91] a district court described the uncertainty of applying *Smith* to neutral civil regulations. Many jurisdictions, noted the court, have interpreted *Smith* as holding that *any* free exercise claim standing alone need only be subject to rational basis review. Other jurisdictions, however (most notably the Ninth Circuit), have limited *Smith*'s holding to free exercise challenges to criminal laws.

The *Big Sandy* case, like *New Rider*, involved several Native American schoolchildren who wished to wear their hair long in violation of their school's dress code. The children and their parents brought claims for violation of their

---

[87] 393 U.S. 503 (U.S. 1969). The Court in *Tinker* held that high school students wearing black armbands to protest the Vietnam War were engaging in protected speech. In order to justify prohibiting the armbands, a school would have to show that allowing them would substantially interfere with the discipline needed to operate the school. The defendants in *Tinker* failed to do this, and the Court struck down their anti-armband policy.
Note that this standard is not actually very different from the one used by the Court of Appeals in *New Rider*. However, that court accepted without proof the school board's claim that the long-hair regulation was necessary to enforce discipline.

[88] *Teterud v. Burns*, 522 F.2d 357 (8th Cir. 1975).

[89] 432 F. Supp. 947 (D. Conn. 1977).

[90] 527 F.2d 492 (2d Cir. 1975).

[91] 817 F. Supp. 1319 (E.D. Tex. 1993).

First Amendment free exercise and free speech rights, as well as their Fourteenth Amendment equal protection and due process rights. An anthropologist testified at trial that many Southeastern Indian tribes traditionally wore their hair long and believed that hair was sacred, but he could not speak about the Alabama Coushatta Tribe specifically because tribal members did not talk to outsiders about their beliefs and rituals. Two of the plaintiff children testified that they believed their long hair was a part of their religion and their Native heritage.

The district court initially noted that, in the Fifth Circuit, school hair-length regulations were not considered a violation of free speech, and were thus subject only to rational basis review.[92] The court also noted that the Fifth Circuit had yet to rule on the scope of *Smith*'s application, and expressed grave misgivings about applying the *Smith* rational basis test to any and all free exercise claims. Thankfully, the court decided, it did not have to do so, because the *Big Sandy* plaintiffs had "a hybrid claim of free exercise, free speech, due process, and equal protection rights."[93] According to the *Smith* majority, when a free exercise claim is paired with a free speech claim, a higher standard of scrutiny is called for. Here, the court found that the plaintiffs had a valid free speech claim under *Tinker*, because the testimony of the plaintiffs and the anthropologist constituted "compelling evidence that long hair in Native American culture and tradition is rife with symbolic meaning."[94] Finally, citing to prison cases like *Teterud* and *Moskowitz*, the court held that, if hair regulations were not narrowly tailored to serve a compelling state interest in prison, they definitely could not be so in the more relaxed environment of public schools.

Long hair, it seems, may be viewed as both a form of religious exercise and a symbolic expression of cultural heritage. What else might fit this description? Dress? Diet? How about the ingestion of peyote in a communal religious ceremony? In the confusing world of post-*Smith* First Amendment jurisprudence, a plaintiff would be well-advised to invoke both religion and expression, and to find an anthropologist who will testify accordingly.

V. Culture Used to Bolster a Plaintiff's Credibility

In the early 1980s, a Hmong man named Vang Xiong Toyed worked for the Washington State Department of Employment Security in Spokane,

---

92 *Citing Karr v. Schmidt*, 460 F.2d 609 (5th Cir. 1972).
93 817 F. Supp. at 1332.
94 *Id.* at 1333.

Washington.[95] His job was to interview refugees and help them to find work. In 1983, Xiong told Yia Moua, a Hmong client from Laos, that he would pick her up and take her somewhere so she could study for her driver's license exam. Instead, he allegedly drove her to a motel and raped her.

That same year, Xiong also allegedly raped Maichao Vang, another Hmong client who had contacted him to help her find a job. Vang testified at trial that Xiong raped her "at least sixteen times," relying each time on the pretext of helping her to find work or to study for her driver's license.[96] Moua and Vang eventually told their husbands about the rapes, and the couples brought a complaint against Xiong under § 1983, alleging that he had used his official position to deprive them of their constitutional right to freedom from sexual assault. A federal jury awarded the plaintiffs $300,000.

On appeal, Xiong argued that there was no evidence supporting the jury's finding that he had acted "under color of state law."[97] The rapes, he asserted, had nothing to do with his authority as a state employee. The appeals court disagreed, citing the testimony of anthropologist Marshall Hurlich, who explained at trial that Hmong refugees rely heavily on government assistance when they come to the United States, and are therefore "in awe of government officials."[98] The court concluded that, based on Hurlich's testimony, the jury could reasonably have found that Xiong used his position at the Department of Employment Security to influence and control the plaintiffs in order to rape them.

Xiong also specifically challenged the district court's admission of Hurlich's testimony. Hurlich, an expert on Hmong culture as well as an epidemiologist at the Seattle Department of Public Health, testified at trial about the cultural roles of Hmong women and the Hmong refugees' awe of American government officials. He described the submissiveness and obedience that are expected of Hmong women, and their attitudes about sex, marriage, and infidelity. Xiong argued that this testimony was not relevant and was prejudicial to his case.

Again, the appellate court did not agree. Hurlich, the court noted, was the only expert that either side had been able to find who could explain Hmong history and culture to the jury. His testimony was relevant to helping the jury understand why the parties behaved as they did. "For example," wrote the

---

[95] The facts of this case are taken from *Vang v. Xiong*, 944 F.2d 476 (9th Cir. 1991).

[96] *Id.* at 478.

[97] *Id.* at 478-79. The appellate court applied the exacting "no evidence" standard because Xiong's attorney failed to move for a directed verdict at the close of the evidence, and was thus precluded from moving for a JNOV after the verdict. With a JNOV, the standard is "sufficient evidence."

[98] *Id.* at 480.

court, "plaintiffs continued to have contact with Xiong after he raped them. Hurlich's testimony regarding the place of Hmong women in that culture was helpful in understanding plaintiffs' actions after Xiong's attacks."[99] The court held that the testimony was indeed prejudicial, because it supported the plaintiffs' claims and their credibility. However, it was not *unduly* so, because it was directly relevant and limited to general statements about Hmong culture.

As the facts of the *Vang* case suggest, this type of cultural credibility evidence can also be used in a criminal context. For example, in *Castillo v. State*,[100] the Texas Court of Appeals affirmed the conviction of Raul Castillo, a *curandero* (faith healer) accused of sexually assaulting a sixteen-year-old girl, O.E., under the pretense of curing her. At trial, the State had introduced testimony from Marie Teresa Hernandez, a doctoral student in cultural anthropology, about the rituals and practices of *curanderos*. On appeal, the court accepted the State's assertion that it had called Hernandez to testify "in order to help the jury understand why impressionable young people like O.E. might feel compelled to comply with the prescriptions of a *curandero*."[101] Castillo did not challenge the relevance of Hernandez's testimony, but only its reliability. The appellate court concluded that it was within the trial court's discretion to admit the testimony.

VI. Cultural Criteria as Part of Statutory Law

In 1984, Marina Rena Katelnikoff and her father shot and skinned approximately 35 sea otters off the coast of Port Lions, Alaska.[102] Katelnikoff had the pelts tanned and then used them to make "stuffed bears, pillows, hats, mittens, and fur flowers which she characterizes as 'cat-tails, pussy willows, and puffs.'"[103] She used some commercial patterns, copied some items that she owned, and also used some of her own designs and those of local craftspeople.

The Marine Mammal Protection Act ("MMPA") governs the taking of marine mammals in U.S. waters. The Act contains an exemption allowing the Indians, Aleuts, and Eskimos of Alaska to kill marine mammals for subsistence or "for purposes of creating and selling authentic native articles of handicrafts and clothing."[104] Katelnikoff was an Aleut, and labeled all of her crafts for sale with silver tags, obtained from the Alaska Department of Commerce and Economic Development, that read "Authentic Native Handicraft from Alaska." However,

---

[99] *Id.* at 482.
[100] 2000 Tex. App. LEXIS 410 (Tex. Ct. App. 2000) (Unpublished).
[101] *Id.* at *4.
[102] The facts of this case are from *Katelnikoff v. United States Dep't of Interior*, 657 F. Supp. 659 (D. Alaska 1986).
[103] *Id.* at 660-61.
[104] *Id.* at 660, *quoting* 16 U.S.C. § 1371(b).

the regulations promulgated to implement the MMPA limit "authentic native articles" to those "which ... were commonly produced on or before December 21, 1972."[105] U.S. Fish & Wildlife Service agents, upon determining that Katelnikoff's crafts did not fit this criterion, seized the items and refused to give them back. Katelnikoff sued.

The primary issue in *Katelnikoff* was whether the regulation Katelnikoff had allegedly violated was consistent with the MMPA and Congressional intent. Katelnikoff argued that the MMPA's exemption was intended to preserve native handicrafts, but that the regulation defeated this purpose by suppressing artistic expression and limiting "native" uses to a time when few, if any, natives were allowed to hunt sea otters, due to restrictive laws and low species numbers. The government argued that the exemption was only intended to preserve native traditions, and that the MMPA's overall purpose of protecting marine mammals would hardly be consistent with expanding native commercial uses of the animals. The court sided with the government, noting Congress's frequent use of words like "traditional" and "cultural legacy" in its testimony and reports on the exemption.

Unfortunately for Katelnikoff, the court was able to use her own evidence against her. Katelnikoff presented two experts, who testified that sea otters had been used in Alaska for a wide variety of purposes long before Russians and Europeans arrived, including parkas, hats, bone tools, bedding, and even children's toys. Presumably, Katelnikoff felt that this testimony would demonstrate that the government's interpretation of "traditional" was too narrow. The court, however, found that the broad range of traditional uses merely indicated that the challenged regulation would not restrict the artistry of native craftspeople. As the natives are forced to "search their cultural pasts for traditional uses," wrote the court rather patronizingly, "they will likely broaden the range of commercial options open to them and expand their creative visions as well."[106]

As *Katelnikoff* demonstrates, attempts to legislate what is "traditional" or "authentic" can result in arbitrary and frustrating legal standards. At least one commentator has pointed out that, while the idea of "tradition" appears with great frequency in Alaskan resource law, the term is rarely defined or explained.[107] This lack of a definition is often just as problematic as an arbitrary or inept one. In *Alaska State Snowmobile Ass'n v. Babbitt,*[108] for example, the plaintiff Association sued various governmental agencies for the right to use

---

105 *Id., quoting* 50 C.F.R. § 18.3.

106 *Id.* at 667.

107 Tomsen, Jennifer L. "Note: 'Traditional' Resource Uses and Activities: Articulating Values and Examining Conflicts in Alaska." 19 Alaska L. Rev. 167 (2002).

108 79 F. Supp. 2d 1116 (D. Alaska 1999).

snowmobiles in Denali National Park. While the Alaska National Interest Lands Conservation Act allowed snowmobile access to restricted conservation areas for "traditional activities," the court had a terrible time trying to figure out what the U.S. National Park Service considered to be "traditional." With no official standard, the court was compelled to find that the closure of the Park to snowmobiling was arbitrary and capricious.

Laws that treat culture as a dynamic and complex feature of daily life, instead of a relic in need of pristine preservation, are likely to do a better job of respecting the needs of people and communities. For example, every voting district in Alaska is required to be "as nearly as practicable a relatively socio-economically integrated area."[109] In *Hickel v. Southeast Conference*, the plaintiffs challenged the Alaska Governor's 1991 redistricting plan as violative of this constitutional mandate. The court admitted the testimony of local residents and anthropologists about the socio-economic relationships prevailing in particular areas, and proceeded to adjust the district boundaries accordingly. Though the term "socio-economically" is not very different from "culturally," perhaps the former's overtones of modern life and everyday concerns make it more conducive to practical decision-making than the latter, with its hint of museum exhibits and colorful national costumes.

VII. The Presentation of Cultural Evidence

In some cases, such as the *Yang* case discussed in Section IV, the court will accept the plaintiffs' own assertions about their beliefs and culture without further evidence. Often, however, expert testimony is helpful or necessary to support the plaintiffs' stated beliefs, or to respond to a defendant's charge of prevarication. For example, in the *Friedman* case discussed in Section II, the defense challenged Friedman's beliefs and Rabbi Stahl's interpretation of Hebrew law. The court held that the rabbi's testimony was not supposed to demonstrate the correct interpretation of Hebrew law, but only "whether there is a branch of Judaism which believes in this interpretation; and, whether Miss Friedman is a member of this group."[110] Rabbi Stahl's testimony answered yes to both questions, and provided a context for understanding Friedman's motivations when she jumped from the ski lift.

So what exactly is "expert" testimony? In 1993, the Supreme Court decided the case of *Daubert v. Merrell Dow Pharmaceuticals, Inc.*,[111] which set the modern standard for the admission of expert testimony. The Court's standard is based

[109] *Hickel v. Southeast Conference*, 846 P.2d 38, 43 (Alaska 1992), *quoting* Alaska Const. art. VI, § 6.
[110] 54 Misc. 2d at 452-53.
[111] 509 U.S. 579 (1993).

on the Federal Rules of Evidence, which allow "a witness qualified as an expert by knowledge, skill, experience, training, or education" to testify in situations where his or her "specialized knowledge will assist the trier of fact to understand the evidence or to determine a fact in issue."[112] The "qualified as an expert" requirement is to ensure that the testimony is reliable, while the "assist the trier of fact" requirement ensures that it is relevant. The *Daubert* court went on to describe some factors for courts to consider when evaluating the reliability of scientific testimony, which was the kind at issue in that case.

Though anthropology and related disciplines are not "hard sciences," the general outlines of the *Daubert* test can still be applied to experts on culture. The court in *Castillo*, discussed in Section V, gave some good guidelines for evaluating the reliability of testimony derived from the social sciences. The court began by noting that the validity of the witness's "technique" or "theory" is not usually the issue in social science, as it is in hard science. Instead, the court suggested three factors to consider. First, is the expert's area of expertise legitimate? Anthropology passes this test, as would probably any social science taught at major universities. Astrology does not. Second, is the expert testifying to matters "within the scope of that field"?[113] Though cultural evidence is generally within the scope of cultural anthropology, a more narrow focus is likely to be much more persuasive than a general one. For example, the anthropologist in *Castillo* taught courses at the University of Houston on Mexican-American culture, and had spent over two years interviewing people involved with *curandero* practice and reading about similar practices. Third, is the expert properly relying on the principles of his or her discipline? This may be difficult to discern for anthropology, but experts should at least be able to cite the sources of their information.

The expert witness reports offered in *Recreational Dev. of Phoenix, Inc. v. City of Phoenix*[114] provide a good example of how *not* to present expert cultural testimony. The *Phoenix* plaintiffs were various owners and patrons of "swingers" clubs in the Phoenix area who sought to prevent the City from enforcing its ordinance against sex clubs. The City claimed that the ordinance was intended to combat the spread of sexually transmitted diseases. The plaintiffs attempted to portray swingers as a responsible, safe, and expressive "subculture" whose clubs posed no STD risk. In support of this contention, the plaintiffs submitted reports by two putative experts, Dr. Norman Scherzer and Terry Gould.

First, the court considered the legitimacy of the experts' fields. Dr. Scherzer's "field" could not be identified. His report stated that he had a Ph.D., but did

---

112 *Id.* at 588, quoting FRE 702.

113 2000 Tex. App. LEXIS 410 at *7.

114 220 F. Supp. 2d 1054 (D. Ariz. 2002).

not say what area the degree was in or from where it was obtained. The Gould report identified Gould as an investigative journalist. Second, the court considered whether the reports offered testimony within the experts' scope of expertise. This was impossible to say for Dr. Scherzer, who had no identifiable field. For Gould, the answer was no. Gould may have been an accomplished investigative reporter, but "[h]e was not trained as a sociologist or anthropologist, academic disciplines that *might* qualify one to provide reliable information about the particular cultural traits and behavior patterns of a particular group of people."[115] Third, the court looked at the experts' methods. Dr. Scherzer's methods seemed unreliable for any field, as his report relied on anecdotal evidence (which he referred to as "antidotal"), unsupported statistical assertions, and uncited professional journals. Gould also seemed to lack any sort of professional methodology. He claimed to have "inspected" the plaintiffs' clubs, but did not say when, how often, or whether he identified himself as an investigative journalist to the clubs' employees. Gould and Dr. Scherzer both claimed to rely on other experts' studies, but did not cite to any sources that could be checked or evaluated. The court found that both expert reports were inadmissible under *Daubert*, and ordered them both stricken.

VIII. Protecting Indigenous Culture

On the island of Mata Nui, the Tohunga are struggling. Their heroes, whom the Tohunga call the Toa, must fight an evil creature named Makuta in order to liberate their island. This may sound to some ears like the beginning of a fantastical Polynesian legend, and in a way, it is. But this legend was told recently by a large Danish toy company, and its characters are all made of colorful plastic blocks.

The Tohunga and their imperiled island were created by Lego as part of a popular computer game/toy line called Bionicle. In 2001, shortly after the game was released, a New Zealand lawyer named Maui Solomon sent a letter to Lego on behalf of three Maori tribes. The Maori were offended by the game's use of Maori words and names, and concerned that Lego intended to claim legal rights to these words. They demanded that Lego stop selling Bionicle.[116] Lego met with Maori representatives in New Zealand and the parties came to an agreement, under which Lego changed the most offensive Maori names (namely "Tohunga," which is usually defined as "priest" or "healer"—not a word to be taken lightly), stopped using Maori words for new characters, and pledged to develop a code of conduct for future use of traditional cultural

[115] *Id.* at 1062, quoting *Jinro Am., Inc. v. Secure Invs., Inc.*, 266 F.3d 993, 1006 (9th Cir. 2001).
[116] "Lego game irks Maoris," BBC News, May 31, 2001.

elements.[117] Despite the agreement, a group of Maori computer hackers attacked an independently-run Bionicle fan website, prompting retaliatory attacks by the site's users on a Maori activist website.[118]

At the heart of this small struggle lies an increasingly important question: Should elements of a culture—words, symbols, designs, dances, medical knowledge—be treated as property? In October 2000, the World Intellectual Property Organization (WIPO), a UN agency, established the Intergovernmental Committee on Intellectual Property and Genetic Resources, Traditional Knowledge and Folklore (IGC) in order to answer this question. The IGC has yet to forge an international consensus on the issue, though it has researched the needs of "traditional knowledge holders" in 28 countries[119] and developed draft provisions for member states to use in formulating their own cultural protection laws.[120]

If the purpose of intellectual property (IP) law is to provide a financial incentive or reward for individual creativity, then it would seem to be a bad fit for traditional knowledge, which is shaped by many individuals over long periods of time and for reasons that transcend the financial. In this view, IP protection for traditional knowledge goes too far, because it restricts the use of certain information (the downside of IP protection) but will not stimulate the creation of new information (the usual justification for IP protection). On the other hand, the consequences of misusing cultural information may also transcend the financial, leading some to argue that regular IP protection for traditional knowledge does not go far enough.

Some recent Australian cases may help to illustrate this dilemma. Australia, a country historically indifferent to the needs of its indigenous population, has taken great strides in the past few decades towards addressing issues of Aboriginal lands and culture.[121] In the area of intellectual property, the courts only began to acknowledge in the late 1980s that Aboriginal artwork could be considered "original" for copyright purposes.[122] By 1994, in the case of *Milpurrurru v. Indofurn Pty. Ltd.*,[123] the Northern Territory court expressed

---

[117] Griggs, Kim. "Lego Site Irks Maori Sympathizer," Wired.com, November 21, 2002. (There seems to be a lot of irking going on.)

[118] Coombe, Rosemary J. and Andrew Herman. "Rhetorical Virtues: Property, Speech, and the Commons on the World-Wide Web," *Anthropological Quarterly*, Volume 77, Number 3, Summer 2004, pp. 559-574.

[119] Report available at <http://www.wipo.int/tk/en/tk/ffm/report/index.html>.

[120] At <http://www.wipo.int/tk/en/consultations/draft_provisions/draft_provisions.html>.

[121] See, generally, Grad, Rachael. "Indigenous Rights and Intellectual Property Law: A Comparison of the United States and Australia," 13 Duke J. Comp. & Int'l L. 203, 209-213 (2003).

[122] Brown, Michael F. *Who Owns Native Culture?*, p. 44. Cambridge: Harvard University Press, 2003.

[123] 54 F.C.R. 240 (1994) (Australia).

surprise that the respondents would even try to contest the copyright ownership of Aboriginal artists. The court found such denial to be an "extraordinary tactical stance," and eventually awarded partial trial costs to the artists for having their time wasted.

The *Milpurrurru* decision (commonly known as the *Carpets* case because the respondents used the artists' designs without permission to decorate carpets) is noteworthy for the serious consideration and respect given to the Aboriginal artists' cultural claims. For example, "[i]n accordance with Aboriginal custom," the court refrained from using the names of the artists who were deceased, and instead referred to them by their "skin names," or kinship group names. More importantly, the court allowed the artists to present cultural evidence to explain the damage caused by the respondents' misappropriation of their artwork. The paintings at issue in the *Carpets* case were of sacred stories and themes, and their clan owners would never have permitted them to be used on carpets for placing on the floor and walking upon. As the artists and other witnesses testified, the right to use a clan's designs, stories, and totemic figures may be entrusted to an individual artist, but that artist is expected to use the material only in ways that are beneficial to the clan. Moreover, the artist is held responsible for any misuse of the material by third persons, even without the artist's consent. Punishment in modern times may include "preclusion from the right to participate in ceremonies, removal of the right to reproduce paintings of that or any other story of the clan, being outcast from the community, or being required to make a payment of money." One witness even mentioned spearing as a punishment in "serious cases."

Like the plane crash victims discussed in Section II, the Aboriginal artists had fairly straightforward tort claims (wrongful death in the former cases; copyright violations here), and only used cultural evidence to illustrate the extent of their damages. The court found that Australia's Copyright Act could address the cultural harm by way of additional damages for personal humiliation and suffering (including "[a]nger and distress suffered by those around the copyright owner") and flagrant infringement, as well as a catch-all provision directing courts to consider "all other relevant matters."[124] After much discussion, the court awarded $5000 to each of the artists for the flagrancy of the infringement, plus an additional $10,000 to each of the still-living artists for "the harm suffered . . . in their cultural environment."

Just four years after the *Carpets* case, George Milpurrurru, one of the artists in that case, became involved in a similar case with even wider legal implications. The painting at issue in *Bulun Bulun and Milpurrurru v. R & T Textiles Pty. Ltd.*[125]

[124] Copyright Act 1968 (Cth), s115(4)(b).
[125] 41 I.P.R. 513 (1998); 1998 AUST FEDCT LEXIS 649.

was painted by an Aboriginal artist named Johnny Bulun Bulun, and used without permission by the respondent textile company for decorating clothing fabrics. Perhaps taking a lesson from the *Carpets* case, which was heard by the same judge, the respondent in *Bulun Bulun* did not attempt to deny the copyright infringement, choosing instead to plead ignorance and quickly settle with Bulun Bulun. This left only Milpurrurru's claim: that, given the nature and customs of Aboriginal artwork, the entire Ganalbingu clan should be considered equitable owners of the painting and its copyright. As Justice Von Doussa succinctly noted at the outset of his opinion, "These proceedings represent another step by Aboriginal people to have communal title in their traditional ritual knowledge, and in particular in their artwork, recognised and protected by the Australian legal system."

Because Milpurrurru's claim was based on Ganalbingu cultural norms, the court was obliged to consider the role of Aboriginal customary law in the Australian legal system. A close reading of Von Doussa's brief but fascinating discussion of this issue reveals the truly revolutionary nature of this case. Von Doussa cites a number of recent cases holding that native customs are irrelevant to (or at least difficult to reconcile with) Western-style jurisprudence, including more than one case from the High Court. However, he then brings up the High Court's own decision in *Mabo v The State of Queensland [No 2]*,[126] a watershed 1992 case in which the Court ruled that Aboriginal Australians retained native title in their ancestral lands under Australian common law. The Court's decision, Von Doussa points out, required legal recognition of Aboriginal laws and customs that predate the Crown's acquisition of the territory of Australia. This is a "clear example" that "[e]vidence of customary law may be used as a basis for the foundation of rights recognised within the Australian legal system." He then goes on to cite one more clear example: his own decision in the *Carpets* case!

After establishing the admissibility of the cultural evidence, the court headed straight into Bulun Bulun's affidavit. In it, the painter describes the waterhole depicted in his painting, the importance of the site to the Ganalbingu people, and the role of painting, ceremony, and ritual in maintaining the clan's connection to their land. He concludes that reproduction of the painting without permission amounts to interference with the clan members' relationship to the land and to their creator ancestors. This testimony was confirmed by Milpurrurru and Djardie Ashley, another clan artist and advisor to Bulun Bulun. Ashley also explained that mass commercial reproduction of such a painting would require unanimous agreement from all of the traditional clan owners of the right to make the painting, and that "Bulun Bulun could not act alone to permit the reproduction of [the painting] in the manner as was done."

[126] 175 CLR 1 (1992); 1992 AUST HIGHCT LEXIS 86.

Further supporting evidence was given by two anthropology professors who had "conducted extensive research into the cultures of the peoples of eastern Arnhem Land [where the Ganalbingu people reside]."

While Milpurrurru's evidence clearly showed that the Ganalbingu people were deeply affected by the treatment of the painting, how could this be addressed by the Australian common law? The court considered a number of possible avenues, including communal title in the painting and equitable ownership rights for the clan in Bulun Bulun's copyright. While the first was not compatible with Australian law and the second was not justified by the facts, the court did find that a fiduciary relationship existed between Bulun Bulun and the Ganalbingu clan. Interestingly, the court found common-law precedent for this in the case law of the country of Ghana, where tribal leaders are considered fiduciaries of their tribes in their handling of tribal property. Bulun Bulun's fiduciary obligation to his clan was "not to exploit the artistic work in a way that is contrary to the laws and custom of the Ganalbingu people, and, in the event of infringement by a third party, to take reasonable and appropriate action to restrain and remedy infringement of the copyright in the artistic work." Because Bulun Bulun had fulfilled this obligation in the present case, the court found that no further action was needed. However, the court went on to state that, in future situations, if a fiduciary like Bulun Bulun were to fail to take the appropriate remedial actions, the court would be willing to intervene, and would even consider (if necessary) imposing a constructive trust on a copyright for the benefit of a clan.

These Australian cases reveal some of the great difficulties a judicial system may face in using Western intellectual property laws and concepts to prevent cultural harm. On the one hand, it would be unfair, or at least unrealistic, to expect non-indigenous people to know or be bound by traditional indigenous laws and customs. On the other hand, it would seem a tremendous injustice to allow any continuing offense or disrespect to indigenous cultures like the Ganalbingu, who have already suffered so much harm at the hands of outsiders. A casual observer might throw his hands in the air and conclude that the demands of IP law and the needs of traditional cultures are simply irreconcilable. But in the careful, thorough, yet trailblazing jurisprudence of Justice Von Doussa, we can see another conclusion—that the two can be reconciled if we are willing to do the work. We do not need to grant special rights to certain groups, or to incorporate traditional indigenous customs into the common law. We need only open our courtrooms to the presentation of appropriate cultural evidence, and open our ears to voices different from our own.

IX. Conclusion

Plaintiffs may use cultural claims and evidence in myriad different ways. Culture may be used to explain why a plaintiff behaved in a certain way, as with Ruth Friedman and Maichao Vang. It may also help a factfinder to understand why an event was especially damaging to a plaintiff, as in the plane crash cases and the Australian *Carpets* case. Cultural claims may be described as the exercise of religion or symbolic speech for First Amendment purposes, as with the Yangs, the Kickapoo Tribe, and the Church of the Lukumi Babalu Aye. Cultural elements may be written into statutory law, forcing plaintiffs like Marina Rena Katelnikoff to litigate the validity and authenticity of their own cultural expressions.

In multicultural societies, we try to teach our children that it is important to respect different cultures and traditions. American first-graders now learn about Hanukkah and Kwanzaa during the winter months, while high-schoolers read novels by African and Asian writers. But full respect is not always easy, because it may involve acknowledging the arbitrariness or subjectivity of our own practices and beliefs. Whether or not we eat the meat of cows, wear our hair long, autopsy our dead, or retain strong bonds with our extended families, we often assume without question the correctness of our own ways of thinking and living, making it difficult to fully accept other ways of doing things.

Alison Renteln concludes *The Cultural Defense* with a plea for jurists to consider cultural evidence as a regular, systematized part of the legal process. Essentially, her argument is that culture shapes minds, and mental states determine culpability. I agree with Renteln that courts should be required to consider cultural evidence, but for much broader reasons than determining the culpability of criminal defendants. Whether presented by a criminal defendant or a civil plaintiff, cultural evidence forces us to confront our assumptions about how people should behave. In law, as in science, we cannot come to sound conclusions without recognizing the assumptions we have made along the way.

Must courts decide whether one culture or belief has more validity, more truth, than another? As many disappointed plaintiffs have discovered, the courtroom is not generally a place for discovering objective truth. It is only a place for resolving disputes. But if we give serious consideration to cultural evidence and the life stories behind it, if we do the difficult work of trying to understand other points of view, if we can humble ourselves enough to acknowledge that our own ways of thinking do not represent absolute truth, we might come closer to resolving our disputes in a way that does justice to the subjective truth in each of us.

AN EXAMINATION INTO THE INFLUENCE OF FRANZ KAFKA ON AMERICAN JURISPRUDENCE

Jonathan Blackmore[1]
Shepard Broad Law Center
Nova Southeastern University

This paper seeks to explore and explain some of the key ways in which judicial opinions in the United States cite the works of the 20th century author Franz Kafka. A Westlaw search shows that the name "Franz Kafka" appears in 54 federal and state court opinions. "Kafkaesque" is used in 363 federal and state court opinions. "The Trial" appears in 207 cases in the same paragraph as "Kafka."

There are two principal contexts in which Kafka is used in judicial opinions. It should be noted that these contexts often blend together and are not necessarily distinguishable. The first context involves any deprivation of due process. In such cases, Kafka's novel *The Trial* is cited, too, and a circumstance of the main character, Joseph K., is usually compared analogously to the situation of the individual who is deprived of due process. These cases may involve police or government abuse of an individual's civil rights, or a violation of the rules of court.

The term "Kafkaesque," in the second context, is used to illustrate a scenario in which a government rule, or rules at issue, is needlessly complex to the point of being illogical. These situations can involve an individual overwhelmed by a web of government regulations, such as an immigrant trying to avoid deportation.[2] "Kafkaesque" is most frequently used to describe arbitrary use of government power, and can be used to characterize an argument as illogical.

These two contexts can blend together, because when a person is deprived of due process, as in the case of Joseph K. in *The Trial*, it may also be "Kafkaesque" in the sense that the individual is incapable of defending himself against an arbitrary and overwhelming government. The term "Kafkaesque" is also defined as "of Kafka," "or relating to his work."[3] Therefore, the circumstance of Joseph K. is by definition, "Kafkaesque."

---

[1] Jonathan Blackmore, JonathanB31@aol.com. 2410 Brickell Avenue #104C, Miami, Florida USA 33129.

[2] *Singh v. Reno*, (1999) 182 F. 3d 504, 510 (7th Cir.)

[3] "Kafkaesque." Merriam-Webster Online Dictionary. 2008. Merriam-Webster Online. 9 November 2008. <http://www.merriam-webster.com/dictionary/Kafkaesque>

The Use of *The Trial*

In *The Trial*, [4] the protagonist, Joseph K., is arrested one morning without warning and without being informed of his crime. Throughout the story, K., although allowed to go about his normal routine, attempts in vain to defend himself. His trial and all related proceedings take place in secret without his participation, and the more he seeks to learn about his case, the more confounded he becomes. He is faced with a senselessly complex, farcical legal system in which he is forced to confront an endless number of low-ranking bureaucrats, none of whom are able to inform him of his crime. Throughout, he assumes that his arrest is a mistake because he has not committed a crime. However, his trial moves forward with an unstoppable momentum. In one of the more famous episodes, K. is wandering throughout a large tenement house hopelessly searching for the courtroom in which his "initial inquiry" is to take place. When he finds the courtroom, the Examining Magistrate is so uninformed that he believes K. to be a house painter. The story culminates with K. being taken away by two executioners, led to a quarry, and put to death. At no point in the story is he informed of his crime.

The Trial is one of the most analyzed works of 20th century literature. The story and its author are unique in many aspects. Notably, Kafka did not complete *The Trial*; its chapters were arranged posthumously by Kafka's friend, Max Brod.[5] Kafka was a German-educated, secular Jew who lived in the Czech Province of the Austro-Hungarian Empire.[6] Kafka was educated in the law and worked for a state-run insurance institute in the area of risk-assessment.[7] His writing style, described by literary critics as concise and unpretentious, invites a wide array of interpretations.[8]

The Trial and other works of Kafka are seen by some critics as anticipating the Nazi regime and the horror of Gestapo arrests.[9] The circumstance of Joseph K. is also easily compared to the sham trials carried out by any number of totalitarian regimes. Other critics see the trial of Joseph K. as being reflective of the guilt that Kafka felt in his own life for cutting off his engagement with his fiancée, as well his struggles as a writer.[10] For some judges in modern

[4] Franz Kafka, *The Trial* (first published 1925, 1998 ed).
[5] Angel Flores and Homer Swander, *Franz Kafka Today* (1977). p. 127.
[6] Meno Spann, *Franz Kafka*, (1976). p. 17.
[7] George Dargo, 'Reclaiming Franz Kafka, Doctor of Jurisprudence' (2007) 45 *Brandeis L.J.* 495, 496.
[8] Angel Flores and Homer Swander, *Franz Kafka Today* (1977). p. 145.
[9] Meno Spann, Franz Kafka, (1976). p. 98.
[10] Stanely Corngold, *Franz Kafka The Necessity of Form* (1988). p. 239-241.

American jurisprudence, *The Trial* serves as a compelling example of how a corrupt judicial system can confound and overwhelm a helpless defendant.

The Trial is often used by Judges to give effect to opinions of cases in which individuals are victimized by government. In *B.B. v. Department of Children and Family Services,*[11] two children were removed from the custody of their mother after the death of a sibling. The mother filed a demand for a trial on the dependency proceeding, but the trial was denied indefinitely pending the investigation into the death by the Sheriff's Office, which had admitted that its investigation was at a stalemate.[12] The situation of the mother was worsened by the denial of her discovery request for information pertaining to the death of her child, on the grounds that it pertained to an ongoing criminal investigation.[13]

The Court described the case as a "tragic Kafkaesque scenario," where a mother's children were taken away without her being afforded a trial or given an opportunity to examine the evidence held against her.[14] It quoted the following passage from *The Trial*, which describes the nature of the proceeding against Joseph K.:

"In no other Court was legal assistance so necessary. For the proceedings were not only kept secret from the general public, but from the accused as well. Of course only so far as this was possible, but it had proved possible to a very great extent. For even the accused had no access to the Court records, and to guess from the course of an interrogation what documents the Court had up its sleeve was very difficult, particularly for an accused person, who was himself implicated and had all sorts of worries to distract him."[15]

The Court is able to draw upon the horror that K. faces as a result of being kept in the dark from the charges and evidence held against him. K.'s 'trial' is the hellish ordeal of being an accused living with the threat of conviction, imprisonment or worse for no stated reason.[16]

In *In re J.M.*, a woman was involuntarily committed to a psychiatric care hospital on the basis of a defective warrant.[17] A court then ordered her held for

---

[11] (1999) 731 So. 2d 30, 32-33 (Fla. 4th DCA)
[12] Id.
[13] *Id.* at 32.
[14] *Id.* at 33.
[15] Id.
[16] Robert B. Kershaw, 'Kafka's The Trial: An Enigma Encountered' (2008) 41 DEC Md. B.J. 66, 70.
[17] (1996) 454 Pa. Super. 276, (PA. Super. Ct.).

an additional 90 days without conducting a hearing on the evidence that supported the extended commitment.[18] The Appellate Court held that her due process rights were violated when the commitment was extended without an independent review of the evidence being conducted by the trial Court.[19]

The Court stated that "to her, the experience of the literary figure, Joseph K. became very real."

"You can't go out, you are arrested." "So it seems," said K. "But what for?" he added. "We are not authorized to tell you that. Go to your room and wait there. Proceedings have been instituted against you, and you will be informed of everything in due course."[20]

The Court was able to use the arrest of Joseph K. analogously to the situation of the women whose involuntary commitment was being extended without an independent review of the evidence supporting the commitment. Both K. and the woman were deprived of their freedom by an external, impersonal force in a seemingly unorthodox manner.

In *The Trial*, K. is visited in his room on the morning of his thirtieth birthday by two warders, and—still in bed—is told he is under arrest.[21] He is puzzled by the event because the warders refuse to identify themselves as public officials, and initially believes the matter to be a joke.[22] However, the arrest marks the end of his personal freedom.

In *Rafeedie v. INS*, the U.S. Immigration and Naturalisation Service (INS) used a "special summary proceeding" to exclude a permanent resident from re-entry into the United States.[23] The Attorney General relied upon confidential information and issued an order of exclusion and deportation without allowing Rafeedie an opportunity to cross-examine witnesses, to consider the government's evidence, or to appeal the decision.[24] The INS invoked the summary procedure because of allegations that the Rafeedie was a high-ranking member of a terrorist organization. Because the process did not allow him to confront the INS or the evidence against him directly, the District Court

---

18 *Id.* at 289.

19 *Id.* at 289 - 290.

20 *Id.* at 290.

21 Franz Kafka, The Trial (first published 1925, 1998 ed). P. 4.

22 *Id.*

23 (1988) 688 F.Supp. 729 (D.D.C.)

24 *Id.* at 736.

granted Rafeedie a preliminary injunction that barred the government from employing the summary proceeding.[25]

The Appellate Court affirmed the decision of the lower Court and remarked that Rafeedie, like Joseph K. in *The Trial*, was "in the untenable position of being forced to prove that he was not a terrorist in face of the Government's confidential information: It is difficult to imagine how even someone innocent of all wrongdoing could meet such a burden."[26]

The Court in the following case cites to *The Trial*, in the context of a situation in which a discovery rule has been violated, to invoke the unjustness of a situation in which a person is unable to adequately present their case because they have not been allowed to see the evidence held against them. In *Bulen v. Navajo Refining Co., Inc.*, the defendants knowingly violated the rules of discovery by withholding requested documents and falsifying discovery responses.[27] The Court drew upon *The Trial* in order to explain the importance of the rules of discovery:

"In Franz Kafka's short story *The Trial*, the main character K. was arrested for a crime. *See* Franz Kafka, *The Trial* (Willa & Edwin Muirtran., Schocken Books 1984) (1914). K. did not know of what crime he was accused. K.'s struggle, at least in part, was a result of the fact that he could not discover the necessary information to defend his case. During K.'s first interrogation, the following exchange occurred:

Emboldened by the mere sound of his own cool words in that strange assembly, K. simply snatched the notebook from the Examining Magistrate and held it up with the tips of his fingers, as if it might soil his hands, by one of the middle pages so that the closely written, blotted, yellow-edged leaves hung down on either side. "These are the Examining Magistrate's records," he said, letting it fall on the table again. "You can continue reading it at your ease, Herr Examining Magistrate, I really don't fear this ledger of yours *though it is a closed book to me ....*" (emphasis added).[28]

"K.'s attempt to defend himself is, as the Appellants describe it, a "nightmare" because K. is prohibited from accessing information about his case. This is precisely the nightmare discovery rules were developed to alleviate. The purpose of the Montana Rules of Civil Procedure is to "secure the just, speedy, and inexpensive determination of every action." If anyone in this case is guilty

---

25 Id.
26 880 F. 2d 506, 516.
27 (2000) 301 Mont. 195, 196 (Mont.)
28 Id.

of creating a *Kafkaesque* nightmare, it was the Defendants, who refused to comply with the Rules of Civil Procedure and refused to disclose information necessary for the proper preparation of the Plaintiffs' case."[29]

In the scene in which the Court quotes, K. becomes enraged by the Magistrate's inability to provide him with any information regarding his charge. By examining *The Trial* under the theory of reification, under which a concept is treated as an object, the entire legal process that K. is subjected to is mechanical and therefore incapable of taking into account his protestations.[30] When K. presses the Magistrate to answer some of his questions, the Magistrate responds "you are laboring under a great delusion. These gentleman here and myself have no standing whatever in this affair of yours, indeed we know hardly anything about it, I can't even confirm that you are charged with an offense, or rather I don't know whether you are. You are under arrest, certainly, more than that I do not know."[31] The Magistrate's statement demonstrates a blind obedience to authority.[32]

Courts have also found the lack of presence or inadequacy of an interpreter at a criminal trial worthy of comparison to Joseph K. In *Mendiola v. State*, the defendant claimed that he should be granted a new trial because he did not have a competent interpreter during his initial trial.[33] The Court determined that his interpreter was adequate, and the dissenting judge saw fit to explain the importance of a translator for a criminal defendant:

"A defendant who is subjected to ineffective translation must "guess" at what is going on around him. An atmosphere is created where the defendant is hindered in effectively assisting his own defense, a milieu worthy of Kafka but unworthy of this Court's imprimatur:

Naturally, therefore, the records of the case, were inaccessible to the accused and his counsel, consequently one did not know with any precision, what charges to meet; accordingly it could be only by *pure chance* that it contained really relevant matter. Evidence could be *guessed* at from the interrogations. In such circumstances the Defense was naturally in a very ticklish and difficult position." Id. at 166.

---

29 Id.

30 Patrick J. Glen, 'The Destruction and Reification of the Law in Kafka's "Before the Law" and The Trial,' (2007) 17 S. Cal. Interdisc. L.J. 23, 59-60.

31 Id.

32 Id.

33 (1995) 924 S.W. 2d 157 (Tex.App.-Corpus Christi).

Likewise in *U.S. v. Carrion*, the Court stated that "the right to an interpreter rests most fundamentally, however, on the notion that no defendant should face the Kafkaesque spectre of an incomprehensible ritual which may terminate in punishment."[34]

Many courts draw upon the lack of accessibility K. had to his trial. Some critics believe that K.'s role as an outsider is a manifestation of Kafka's status in his own life.[35]
Kafka was a German-educated secular Jew who lived in the Czech Province of the Austro-Hungarian Empire.[36] He did not fully identify with any of the groups—Germans, Czechs, or Jews.[37] Similar to Kafka, K. is an outsider to his trial. He is ignorant of the charges leveled against him, and he is informed that nobody understands the court structure.[38]
The Trial has been cited to where there is the appearance of arbitrariness on the part of the court. In *Mediterranean Const. Co. v. State Farm Fire & Cas. Co.*, the Judge's clerk telephoned both parties on the morning of their hearing to inform them that the movant's motion for summary judgment had been granted and there would be no hearing.[39] Despite this, counsel for both sides appeared, but were denied permission to argue the merits, object to the evidence, or respond to the other side's papers.[40] On appeal, the Appellate Court determined that denying oral argument creates the appearance of impropriety:

"It is in the nightmare world of Franz Kafka's *The Trial* where Josef K. was left wondering, "Where was the Judge whom he had never seen?"[41]

Similarly in *Rose v. Superior Court*, the lower Court denied the defendant an evidentiary hearing on his motion for ineffective assistance of counsel.[42] The Appellate Court determined that the lower Court had merely skimmed over the defendant's petition so quickly that could not have given it proper consideration.[43] It stated that: [the defendant] Rose, like Kafka's condemned prisoner, Josef K., has been left to wonder, "Where was the Judge whom he had never seen?"[44]

---

34 (1973) 488 F. 2d 12, 14 (1st Cir.).
35 Douglas Litowitz, 'Franz Kafka's Outsider Jurisprudence,' (2002) 27 Law and Soc. Inquiry 103.
36 *Id.* at 104.
37 *Id.*
38 *Id.* at 129.
39 (1998) 66 Cal.App.4th 257, 261 (Cal. 4th DCA).
40 Id.
41 *Id.* at 785.
42 (2000) 92 Cal. Rptr. 2d 313 (Cal. App. 2 Dist.).
43 *Id.* at 321.
44 Id.

The excerpt which the Court uses, "where was the Judge whom he had never seen?," is taken from the final scene of the story, in which K. is executed. Some critics believe that K.'s trial was symbolic of Kafka's engagement to Felice Bauer.[45] Kafka felt that Bauer stood in the way of the life he wanted, to spend as much time writing as he pleased.[46] Kafka's trial, it follows, was his engagement to Bauer, and the only relief from the sense of being on trial would come when the death sentence was passed.[47]

Kafka has also been cited when explaining the limits of government intrusion against the individual's right to privacy. In *Creamer v. Raffety*, at issue was a City's blanket policy of conducting both a strip search and a cavity search on any person arrested and held overnight in the City's jail.[48] In holding that the scope of such a policy was overly broad, the Court explained that:

"[Such a policy] creates a Kafkaesque scheme whereby Mr. Creamer or any other misdemeanant could suffer a massive intrusion upon the right to privacy in the future at the hands of law enforcement personnel stretching the limits of their discretion to release and acting on little or no justification."[49] "In *The Trial*, Franz Kafka described the archetypal encounter of the ordinary mortal with the capriciousness and irrationality of modern bureaucracies."[50]

Some critics suggest that Kafka's depiction of a world controlled by a cruel and arbitrary force is traced to his relationship with his domineering father.[51] On one occasion, Kafka describes in a journal entry, the traumatic childhood experience of being carried out on to the balcony by his father and being locked there for hours.[52] Kafka explained the experience as emblematic of his relationship with his father.[53] The act relates to Kafka's work as an arbitrary punishment at the hands of an unchallengeable authority.[54]

In *State v. Palamia*, the defendant was detained illegally and held for 18 hours without being told of the reason for his arrest, and without being allowed to contact anybody.[55] The police later discovered that the defendant had an

45 Ronald Hayman, *Kafka: A Biography* (1981). P. 183-184.
46 *Id.* at 184.
47 *Id.*
48 (1984) 145 Ariz. 34, (Ariz. 2nd Div. App.).
49 *Id.* at 920-921.
50 *Id.* at 921.
51 *Id.* at 184.
52 Ernst Pawell, The Nightmare of Reason: A Life of Franz Kafka (1997). P. 18.
53 *Id.*
54 Ronald Hayman, *Kafka: A Biography* (1981). P. 184
55 (1983) 124 N.H. 333 (N.H.).

outstanding warrant.[56] The Court stated that the probable cause established by the outstanding warrant was the product of the illegal arrest, and "it is antithetical to the principles of a democratic society to seize someone and hold him for 18 hours, while shopping around to see if a reason exists for the detention. *See* Franz Kafka, *The Trial* (1937)."[57]

The Use of the Term: "*Kafkaesque*"

Kafka's vision of a threatening and pointless bureaucracy was first encapsulated in the English word "Kafkaesque," in 1946.[58] *Merriam Webster* defines "Kafkaesque" as meaning "of, relating to, or suggestive of Franz Kafka or his writings; *especially*: having a nightmarishly complex, bizarre, or illogical quality."[59] *Encarta* defines it as "overly complex in seemingly pointless, impersonal, and often disturbing way."[60] Kafka biographer Jeremy Adler states that the adjective "Kafkaesque" "denotes nightmarish situations, an all-pervasive bureaucracy, looming totalitarianism, infinite hierarchies, and a deep existential angst."[61]

Some scholars suggest that the complex and illogical world Kafka creates was influenced by his employment in a semi-governmental insurance company, the Workers' Accident Insurance Institute, in the heavily-bureaucratic Austro-Hungarian Empire.[62] The company was created by broad and ambitious social legislation aimed at regulating relations between capital and labor, as well as the relationship between the State and the worker.[63] The legislation resulted in part, in corruption and inefficiency.[64]

Kafka's principal task at the institute was the processing of employee appeals against the assignment of their firms to certain risk categories, legal information for enterprises, and measures for the prevention of accidents.[65] His work gave

---

56 *Id.* at 336.
57 *Id.* at 338.
58 Klaus Wagenbach and Ritchie Robertson and Ewald Osers, *Kafka, Life and Times* (2003). P. x
59 "Kafkaesque." Merriam-Webster Online Dictionary. 2008. Merriam-Webster Online. 9 November 2008. <http://www.merriam-webster.com/dictionary/Kafkaesque>
60 "Kafkaesque." Encarta World English Dictionary. 2007. Microsoft Corporation. 9 November 2008. <http://encarta.msn.com/dictionary_/kafkaesque.html>
61 Jeremy Adler, *Franz Kafka* (2001). P. 4.
62 Klaus Wagenbach and Ritchie Robertson and Ewald Osers, *Kafka, Life and Times* (2003). P. ix
63 Ernst Pawell, The Nightmare of Reason: A Life of Franz Kafka (1997). P. 183.
64 *Id.*
65 Klaus Wagenbach and Ritchie Robertson and Ewald Osers, *Kafka, Life and Times* (2003). P. 66.

him exposure to questions concerning government, administration, bureaucracy, and the law—themes that are present in *The Trial.*[66]

Some critics suggest that Kafka's prose was developed by writing reports for The Worker's Accident Institute.[67] The precise and distinctive style present in his fictional works is also present in his official reports regarding industrial accidents, injuries and compensation claims.[68] His descriptive precision and awareness of consequences are attributes of both his professional work and his writing.[69] The period in which Kafka worked at the institute was also his most prolific period as a writer.[70]

Kafka was not immune to run-ins with the institute's management despite being highly regarded among fellow employees.[71] Kafka, on one occasion, filed a thorough and well drawn out complaint with the company board of directors (of which there were more than 20), seeking to obtain higher wages for the institute's draftsmen.[72] Such an experience may have helped Kafka depict bureaucracies in his works.

Judges often use the term "Kafkaesque" to paint a bureaucracy, often within a government agency, as arbitrary and oppressive. In *Hunt v. Indiana Family and Social Services*, the owner of a day care center's license was revoked on the basis of an unsubstantiated charge of child abuse.[73] The Agency refused to remove the charge from Hunt's record despite an Administrative Law Judge's order against the Agency.[74] An official with the Agency explained that he did not believe the administrative law judge's decision to control whether the record would be expunged, and instead relied upon the decision of the social worker who determined the charge of abuse to be valid.[75] The Court stated that, "given these circumstances, the Court can understand Mrs. Hunt's feelings of being caught in a *Kafkaesque* nightmare of unchecked bureaucratic power-if the facts are as the Hunts allege."[76]

66 Jeremy Adler, Franz Kafka (2001). . P. 48-49.
67 George Dargo, 'Reclaiming Franz Kafka, Doctor of Jurisprudence' (2007) 45 Brandeis L.J. 495, 496.
68 *Id.* at 510.
69 *Id.* at 514.
70 *Id.* at 509.
71 Ernst Pawell, The Nightmare of Reason: A Life of Franz Kafka (1997). P. 188-189.
72 Reiner Stach, *Kafka, The Decisive Years* (2005). P. 284.
73 (2007) 2007 WL 2349626 (S.D. Ind.)
74 *Id.* at 1.
75 *Id.* at 4.
76 *Id.* at 5.

In *Abdel-Muhti v. Ashcroft*, the U.S. Immigration and Customs Enforcement Agency (ICE) held the petitioner, an alien, in detention for two years pending a final order of deportation.[77] The Agency claimed that it was holding the petitioner because he failed to cooperate with the INS' efforts to remove him.[78] However, the record established that the petitioner had provided the Agency with all the necessary documentation needed to deport him.[79] The Court stated that:

"The record establishes that Petitioner provided ICE with his birth certificate, including his parents' names, and his region of origin, and made substantial efforts to obtain travel documents. Yet in a *Kafkaesque* exchange that began with Petitioner's November 25, 2002 custody review and culminated with a post-hearing request that he complete a form that was completed and submitted to Israel on November 20, 1975, ICE persists in its demand that he produce something more. While ICE is empowered to prosecute and detain those who withhold information, absent some reasonable basis for its apparent suspicion that Petitioner is lying or withholding information, the law does not authorize ICE to continue Petitioner's detention until he supplies answers it likes."[80]

In *Ngwanyia v. Ashcroft*, the petitioners, immigrants who had attained the status of "asylees," brought action asserting, in part, that the government had failed to provide the them with the documentation necessary to allow them to work while in the United States.[81] Federal law provided that the government must authorize the asylees to engage in employment, and to provide the asylees with the documentation to reflect that authorization.[82] An employer could not hire the asyless without the documentation, which was in the form of a simple government document.[83] The Court was not persuaded by the government's responses to the petitioner's claims, and stated:

"In the face of these simple statutory commands, Defendants have established procedures that verge on the *Kafkaesque*. Defendants provide "no one particular form of an endorsement of employment authorization." Rather, the type of document an asylee receives-and the length of time for which it is valid-

[77] (2004) 314 F.Supp.2d 418 (M.D.PA.)
[78] *Id.* at 427.
[79] *Id.* at 430.
[80] *Id.*
[81] (2004) 302 F.Supp. 2d 1076, (D.Minn.).
[82] *Id.* at 1084.
[83] *Id.* at 1097.

depends upon the manner in which the asylee was granted asylum and the district office handling the asylee's request."[84]

In *Family and Social Services Administration v. Boise*, Boise petitioned for a reclassification of his position with the Division of Family and Children that would provide an increase in compensation.[85] The petition was denied by a Hearing Officer, who ruled that the classification of the petitioner's job status was *not* based solely on caseload size, in spite of facts that clearly showed the contrary.[86] The Appellate Court stated that the Respondents are "...exercising uncontrolled discretion in the application of indeterminable standards to facts the relevance of which would be unknown to them. Such actions are so classically arbitrary and capricious as to be *Kafkaesque*."[87]

In *Kurnik v. Department of Health & Rehabilitative Services*, the a disabled person was denied reimbursement of medication by the Department of Health & Rehabilitative Services after a hearing officer determined that she had not timely applied for assistance.[88] Mismanagement on the part of the agency prevented the petitioner's properly filed application from being processed.[89] The Appellate Court stated that "appellant's *Kafkaesque* experience with that agency was characterized by no information, misinformation, unanswered letters, unreturned phone calls, unfulfilled promises, and classic bureaucratic runaround the sum total of which amounted almost to studied indifference if not purposeful neglect on the part of the agency."[90]

In *H & V Engineering Inc., v. Idaho State Board of Professional Engineers and Land Surveyors*, the State Board indefinitely revoked the licenses of the petitioners, Engineers, for "misconduct in the practice of engineering" which constituted "gross negligence."[91] The petitioners claimed that the action of the board violated their right to due process because the board did not adequately warn them as to what conduct would subject them to discipline.[92] The Court determined that the grounds upon which the petitioners were disciplined were unconstitutionally vague because nothing in the statutory definition, board rules

---

84 *Id.* at 1085

85 (1996) 667 N.E. 2d 753 (Ind. App.).

86 *Id.* at 755.

87 *Id.* at 756.

88 (1995) 661 So. 2d 914 (Fla. 1st DCA).

89 *Id.* at 916.

90 *Id.* at 917.

91 (1987) 113 Idaho 646, 647 (Idaho).

92 *Id.* at 649.

or regulations warned the engineers that their acts would subject them to discipline.[93]

The Court explained that "disciplinary standards cannot be kept secret from the professionals or the courts. In this case, the phantom of unknown standards robbed the engineers of notice as to what conduct was proscribed. As stated in another tribunal: "This *Kafkaesque* chain of secrecy is not what the Due Process Clause contemplates."[94]

In *Meadows v. Lewis*, three workers who suffered injuries during employment filed a petition for a writ of mandamus seeking to force the State Worker's Compensation Commissioner to rule on the compensability of a claim within the time frame mandated by law, pay disability awards, and pay attorney's fees.[95] The Court ruled for the petitioners on all counts, stating:

"Attorneys for the petitioners in this case were forced by bureaucratic indifference to lead their clients on a *Kafkaesque* journey through a labyrinth of administrative bungling. Petitions were processed and hearings scheduled for matters upon which determinations had already been made, consequently resulting in proceedings at which only the hearing examiner appeared. Claims were periodically opened, closed, reopened, reclosed, etc., for no cognizable reason other than the commissioner's repeated justification of "clerical error."[96]

Courts often use "Kafkaesque" to characterize an argument as illogical, or one that would lead to an absurd result. In *Petties v. District of Columbia*, a case arising under the Individuals with Disabilities in Education Act, the school district argued that it was not required to give the parents prior notice of the decision to send their children to a different school, because such a move "did not constitute a change in child placement or program" under the Act.[97] The school board then contended that the parents could not challenge the school board's placement of the children because under the Act, a parent must have notice of the placement in order to make a challenge.[98]

The Court concluded that the Act provides the parent the right to challenge any proposed changes in placement in advance of the change taking place and a right to argue that the changes proposed do in fact effect fundamental changes

---

93 *Id.* at 650.
94 *Id.* at 651.
95 (1983) 172 W.VA. 457, 468-469 (W.VA.).
96 *Id.* at 476.
97 (2002) 238 F.Supp. 2d. 114, 124 (D.D.C.).
98 Id.

in the student's educational program.[99] The Court stated that accepting the School Board's premise would lead to an absurd result.[100] "It is disingenuous-indeed, *Kafkaesque* for the defendants to argue that the burden is on the parents first to identify a fundamental change in a student's educational program in order to raise the claim that there has been a change in placement even though DCPS has not provided notice to the parents of the nature of such proposed change."[101]

In *Williams v. Sullivan*, the petitioner brought suit after his petition for social security benefits was denied.[102] The Secretary of Health and Human Services claimed that the decision was simply the dismissal of the petitioner's request for a hearing, and therefore not subject to judicial review under the Social Security Act.[103] The petitioner claimed that his case was subject to judicial review because the action by the Secretary amounted to the reopening of a previous case.[104] However, the Secretary did not believe the action to be a final decision and refused to turn over the transcript which would help determine the nature of the action.[105]

The Court objected to the reasoning of the Secretary: "This Court finds such *Kafkaesque* reasoning remarkable. If one of the purposes of the act administered by the Secretary is to fairly award benefits actually due beneficiaries, it would seem that he would endeavor to review and make available such information as would be reasonably necessary to make such determinations possible. Additionally, government lawyers have a duty to seek justice and to develop a full and fair record."[106]

Incorrect Uses of Kafka

Attorneys and Judges often cite to Kafka incorrectly, in an effort to dramatise an argument. In *U.S. v. Jackson*, a criminal defendant argued that the prison sentence for the offense he was charged with should be based on the amount of cocaine found on his person at the time of his arrest, as opposed to the amount of cocaine he was convicted of distributing.[107] Jackson argued that using the aggregate amount of cocaine he was charged with possessing is

---

99 *Id.*
100 *Id.*
101 *Id.*
102 (2001) 779 F.Supp. 471 (W.D. Mo.).
103 *Id.* at 472.
104 *Id.*
105 Id.
106 Id.
107 (1997) 121 F. 3d. 316, 321 (7th Cir.).

speculative and that basing a prison term on speculation is *Kafkaesque*.[108] The Court stated that "Jackson is hardly in the position of Joseph K. It is clear what offense Jackson was charged with and Jackson was given an opportunity to defend himself against those charges."[109]

One author has written that the liberal use of Kafka in judicial opinions has distorted the meaning of Kafka's works,[110] and may have the consequence of rendering the term meaningless.[111] In a law review essay, Brian Pinaire comments that Kafka has been used to describe the rush of court proceedings to execute prisoners.[112] This use stands in contrast to the conventional understanding of Kafkaesque to describe the slowness and delay of bureaucracy.[113]

Pinaire also notes that Monica Lewinsky's attorney described the lengthy interrogation of his client by FBI agents as Kafkaesque.[114] This description is inappropriate because the interrogations that take place in *The Trial*, in contrast to the standard interrogation conducted by the FBI, are distinct in that they were not conducted in a standard fashion, but were marked by a secretive and obtuse quality.[115]

Conclusion

The Trial is more than just a work of literature, but has served as a powerful warning of the dangers of arbitrary government. Kafka was able to create a compelling and terrifying world in which the government could, seemingly at random, single its citizens out for punishment in the name of the law. This is even more remarkable because Kafka, unlike Orwell, for example, was not political and did not intend for his stories to be parables.[116]

What makes *The Trial* all the more influential is that it is not set in any single nation, during any particular period of time. Its main character is honest, hardworking, and mostly nondescript. He is easily related to by the reader. The

---

108 Id.
109 *Id.*
110 Brian Pinaire, 'The Essential Kafka: Definition, Distention, and Dilution in Legal Rhetoric,' (2007) 46 U. Louisville L. Rev. 113, 151.
111 *Id.* at 152.
112 *Id.* at 148.
113 *Id.*
114 *Id.* at 147.
115 *Id.*
116 Julian Preece, *The Cambridge Companion to Kafka* (2002). P. 131-132.

story's theme transcends cultures and time. The trial of K. is as relevant today as it was when Kafka was alive.

Judges seem to have latched on to Kafka in order to demonstrate what our law is supposed to prevent. Due process and fairness are designed to prevent government over-reaching and abuse. The world of Joseph K. is an unimaginable nightmare. Judges are able to use that nightmare in order to make the point that government transparency and fairness are fundamental in our society. Without these fundamental protections, what is to prevent the average citizen from being victimized by the state?

TEACHING THE LAW OF WRONGS WITHOUT SEARCHING FOR WHAT IS RIGHT

Robert L. McFarland[1]

Learn to do good; Seek justice.[2]

Each year thousands of students enroll in American law schools. Their decision is somewhat surprising considering evidence linking the first year of study in an American law school to a number of harmful physical, mental and emotional side-effects.[3] At orientation, these new students are typically greeted with some version of the following Damoclean admonition: "Look to your right and look to your left; one of the three of you will not be here next year." First-year law students, like enlisted soldiers entering boot camp, dutifully report to their classrooms prepared to "put aside their personal life and health and accept persistent discomfort, angst, isolation, even depression as the cost of becoming a lawyer."[4] Welcome to the legal profession.

Recent reports regarding the condition of the legal profession are similarly disquieting. The legal profession is distinguished from other professional

---

[1] Associate Professor of Law, Faulkner University, Thomas Goode Jones School of Law. I offer my gratitude to my colleague Adam MacLeod for encouraging me to write this essay. I also thank my colleagues who offered helpful comments on earlier drafts and criticisms of my argument. I look forward to continuing this conversation with all of you.

[2] *Isaiah 1:17 (American Standard Version).* After reviewing a draft of this essay, one of my colleagues encouraged me to remember that law school is a trade school and not a seminary. For the sake of clarity, I want to emphasize that I am not arguing that law school, even a religiously affiliated law school like the one at which I teach, is, or should become, a school of theology. I affirm our obligation to prepare our students for service in the legal profession and equip them with all training necessary for effective participation in "the real world". However, the ancient admonition to do good and seek justice applies to all, even law professors. I do argue that our efforts to prepare law students for service in the legal profession would be more effective if we would integrate these ancient words of wisdom into our pedagogical goals.

[3] *See* Lawrence S. Krieger, 'Institutional Denial About the Dark Side of Law School, and Fresh Empirical Guidance for Constructively Breaking the Silence' (2002) 52 *Journal of Legal Education* 112. Professor Krieger argues that legal educators are in denial about the correlation of legal education to negative mental, physical and emotional effects: 'There is a wealth of what should be alarming information about the collective distress and unhappiness of our [law] students and the lawyers they become. We appear to be practicing a sort of organizational denial because, given this information, it is remarkable that we are not openly addressing these problems among ourselves at faculty meetings and in committees, and with our students in the context of courses and extracurricular programs. The negative phenomena we ignore are visible to most of us and are confirmed by an essentially unrebutted body of empirical findings.': at 112.

[4] Ibid at 118.

pursuits by higher rates of substance abuse, depression, anxiety, divorce and suicide.[5] Why? These indicia of professional malcontent are, in part, a result of a widening gap between the legal profession's ideals and the lawyer's actual work. Lawyers recite an oath in order to obtain their license whereby they dedicate themselves to public service and pursuit of the profession's ideals. Many of these lawyers begin churning out work product for clients they have not met in order to meet demanding billable hour requirements set by the partners of their firms. Many lawyers resign themselves to the view that they are merely cogs in the legal machine.[6]

Legal education well prepares law students for long hours and mechanical service. But is legal education equipping students with the ability to find meaning and satisfaction in their work? Are law schools inspiring students to do good work and to seek justice? Or is the legal academy contributing to that which is ailing the profession?

Some will argue that concern for the health of the legal profession is now irrelevant because the legal profession is already dead.[7] Others claim that the profession is in danger of losing its soul.[8] Respect for the profession "seems everywhere on the decline."[9] As a member of the American legal profession, I join those who are saddened by news of the profession's poor health.[10] Why is the profession in decline? There is a growing body of literature linking the legal

[5] *See eg* Patrick J. Schiltz, 'On Being a Happy, Healthy, and Ethical Member of an Unhappy, Unhealthy, and Unethical Profession' (1999) 52 *Vanderbilt Law Review* 871.

[6] For clarity, I am not arguing that the lawyer's work product is, in this setting, actually disconnected from the pursuit of justice. Instead, as will be discussed below, because the young lawyer's law school training did not adequately develop the lawyer's professional identity, many young lawyers faced with this technical, impersonal and often tedious work will easily lose sight of the connection between their work and the pursuit of justice. Others may react more severely and develop a cynical faith whose core tenant is (whether correct or not) that the entire legal process, the entire profession, is a power game in which ideals such as justice are irrelevant. Such realism contributes to the declining health of both the individual lawyer and the profession. For a more comprehensive description of the new cynical faith in the modern law firm *see* Anthony T. Kronman, *The Lost Lawyer: Failing Ideals of the Legal Profession* (1993) 300-14.

[7] *See* Carl T. Bogus, 'The Death of an Honorable Profession' (1996) 71 *Indiana Law Journal* 911.

[8] *See* Kronman, above n. 6 at 1.

[9] Bogus, above n. 5, 912.

[10] As noted in Professor Bogus' work, some observers are celebrating at the profession's wake. Richard Posner, for example, is eager to bury the profession so that he might get on with more intellectually autonomous and scientifically exact analysis without value-laden side constraints. Ibid.

profession's decline in America with the traditional program of legal education provided by American law schools.[11]

In this essay I will argue that the declining health of the American legal profession (and its members) is caused, in part, by the traditional curriculum and pedagogy of the first year of education in an American law school. Specifically, I will argue that the traditional first year curriculum inappropriately neglects careful examination of moral and legal philosophy as well as professionalism and ethics in order to cultivate an unbalanced, supposedly objective, analytical tough-mindedness lacking moral grounding or constraint. Most law schools intentionally train first year law students to detach themselves from their own moral and ethical identities in order to learn what the law is without being distracted by what they think it ought to be. This process is, in part, necessary and beneficial.[12] However, as Roger Cramton observed while serving as Dean of Cornell Law School, the process is also "dangerous and crippling" if not balanced out by other pedagogical and curricular objectives.[13] I will argue that the traditional first year of legal education is now unbalanced and destructive. The first-year curriculum sharpens minds but dulls souls. The current curriculum and pedagogy transforms the entering student's idealism and desire for engaging in the pursuit of justice into a peculiar sort of realism typified by the fierce skepticism endemic to the practice of law in America today.[14] The remedy, I argue, is balancing the first year curriculum with the integration of a course (preferably the first semester) dedicated to the study of the concept of law and the lawyer's role in the legal system. Those teaching this course would pursue pedagogical objectives much different from the other doctrinal courses in order to provide greater exposure to the relationship between law and justice.[15]

---

[11] William M. Sullivan, Anne Colby, Judith Welch Wegner, Lloyd Bond and Lee S. Shulman, *Educating Lawyers* (2006) (hereinafter referred to as "Carnegie Report"); American Bar Association Section of Legal Education and Admissions to the Bar, *Legal Education and Professional Development – An Educational Continuum: Report of the Task Force on Law Schools and the Profession: Narrowing the Gap* (1992) (hereinafter referred to as "MacCrate Report"); Roy Stuckey, *Best Practices for Legal Education: A Vision and Road Map* (2007).

[12] *See* below n. 26 and related text.

[13] Roger C. Cramton, 'Ordinary Religion of the Law School Classroom' (1977) 29 *Journal of Legal Education* 247, 253.

[14] One study conducted by a group of psychologists at the University of Arizona and discussed by Professor Krieger in his research, found that law students entered law school with normal psychological markers but quickly shifted to major psychological distress in the first year. Krieger, above n. 3 at 114 (citation omitted).

[15] Some will undoubtedly argue that this proposal is yet another "academic" solution to a problem requiring more creative, non-traditional solutions. I respond to this argument below.

I will begin by describing the traditional method of legal education utilized in the first year at American law schools giving particular attention to the study of tort law. In this section, we will follow a first-year student through her first few weeks in torts starting with her purchase of *Prosser on Torts* and then through her first few Socratic discussions. This section will describe the moral dilemma resulting from the first few weeks of the traditional first year curriculum and pedagogy. This dilemma is best summarized in this manner: the first year sharpens the student's ability to identify difficult moral and ethical issues embedded in legal disputes but does not adequately equip the law student to appreciate how these conflicts are resolved within a legal system[16] nor allow the student to reconcile such conflicts with their own presuppositions. Instead, the student is trained to identify legal arguments, find the "rule of law" and move on to the next hard case without carefully reconciling the rule of law with the student's present understanding of justice. Because this process occurs in each of the doctrinal first year courses, without the aid of a contemporaneous examination of legal philosophy, the law student acquires a skewed view of the nature of law and the legal process. Without pursuing an understanding of the nature of law, the competing conceptions of justice and the lawyer's role in a legal system, the law student often acquires the skeptic's belief that there are no right answers to *any* questions (moral, ethical or legal) and the cynic's view that the only outcome-determinative issue in any legal conflict is which party was able to afford "the best" lawyer.[17]

Following this illustrative description of the typical first year experience, I will argue the American legal academy's traditionally unbalanced first-year pedagogy results from a misunderstanding of admonitions regarding legal education given

[16] I am not suggesting that the lawyer is required to resolve every moral or ethical question embedded in a legal dispute. Instead, law students lacking grounding in legal philosophy will not appreciate the distinct roles of lawyers, legislators and judges. They will often assume, on the basis of the Socratic dialogue intended to develop the skill of identifying arguments for each party's use in the adversarial legal system and not intended to examine the merits of or roles within that adversarial system, that moral and ethical questions are not resolvable but by the arbitrary exercise of judicial or legislative power.

[17] As discussed in more detail below, I am not asserting that every case examined in the first year of law school presents a question requiring discussion of what ought to be. Not every legal issue has only one right answer, and reasonable judges or legislators might differently resolve most legal issue. I am arguing that many of the legal rules examined in torts (and other doctrinal first year courses) do rest on premises rooted in moral or legal philosophy. Without an explicit acknowledgement of this reality (a rare occurrence within the Socratic classroom) the average law student forms a conception of law as nothing but what the judge in the case under review arbitrarily declares it to be. There are no right answers. According to Professor Daniel Coquillette, this confusion is at the heart of professional angst. *See* 'Professionalism: The Deep Theory' (1994) 72 *North Carolina Law Review* 1271, 1272.

in Oliver Wendell Homes' influential lecture, *The Path of the Law*. I will argue that Holmes acknowledged the necessity of connecting the particular with the general in order to master the lawyer's trade.

In the final part I will propose a modest change to the first year curriculum and pedagogy: the integration of a new course called *Law, the Lawyer and Justice* in the first semester of study. This course would introduce the law student to the nature of law and differing general theories of justice and also discuss the lawyer's professional obligations to client, bench and bar. This course, I argue, would enhance the student's ability to better develop the analytical skill being imparted by the case method by alleviating the moral tension ordinarily experienced in curriculum lacking an introductory exposure to legal philosophy. My course proposal is not entirely novel. I will identify examples of similar first-year curricular reforms already adopted in the American academy. Finally, as a faculty member at a religiously affiliated law school, I will discuss the relationship of my proposal to recent discussions regarding the role of religiously affiliated law schools in the legal academy.

I. The Traditional First Year Experience in an American Law School: The Loss of Moral Identity

Many students enter law school eager to pursue justice. This, in part, explains why there is a unique, almost palpable, energy present in first-year classrooms in American law schools. Despite their knowledge that law school will be difficult, many first year students are eager to study law. Any professor privileged to teach in the first-year will acknowledge the rich mixture of anxiety, anticipation and expectation in the first-year classroom. Like engines primed with fuel, first-year students expect the study of law to ignite a passion for life in the law.

I teach torts in our first-year curriculum and very much enjoy the energy in the first year classroom. I also teach two upper-division courses and find the students in the upper division much different. Something has changed. Any professor who teaches both first year and second and third year students will recognize this difference. By the time a student reaches their second year, the anxiety of their first year is replace by the sort of self-confidence possessed by one who thinks she has figured out how to play a game. The first year's eagerness to examine the nature of law and justice is often replaced by a resignation to a supposed realism, gleaned from their first year experience, a belief that law is nothing more than legal method used to mask the exercise of power. With the help of career services offices at law schools throughout the academy, second year students spend much more time pursuing employment in the business of law than they do contemplating the moral, social and ethical issues related to the profession's nexus with the pursuit of justice. It is difficult, in this context, to capture the imagination of the student. In many ways, their imagination has already been suppressed.[18]

What happened between the beginning of the first year and the beginning of the second year? The first year happened. The American legal academy is beginning to acknowledge that something in the first year of legal education is broken. For example, the recently released *Best Practices for Legal Education* report concludes that "[t]he first year curriculum gives students a skewed and inaccurate vision of the legal profession and their roles in it. . . . The first year experience as a whole, without conscious and systematic efforts at counterbalance, tips the scales, as Llewellyn put it, away from cultivating the humanity of the student and toward the student's re-engineering into a 'legal machine.'"[19] These concerns are reinforced by the conclusions of the American Bar Association's task force on law schools: "Too often, the Socratic method of teaching emphasizes qualities that have little to do with justice, fairness and morality in daily practice. Students too easily gain the impression that wit, sharp responses, and dazzling performances are more important than the personal moral values that lawyers must possess and that the profession must espouse."[20] These statements are illustrative of a growing recognition within the profession and academy that something is broken in our first year curriculum.

The traditional first year curriculum is doctrinal, analytical and supposedly scientific. The traditional first year experience is antagonistic to the entering student's desire to pursue answers to conceptual questions (i.e., development of an understanding of general theories of justice). The student enrolled in a traditional first year program is not permitted to enroll in legal philosophy. Instead, first years are shoved into multiple doctrinal courses (usually torts, contracts, property, criminal law and civil procedure) alongside one technical skills course (usually legal research and writing).[21] Thus, entering law students

---

[18] For another perspective on this pattern *see* 'Making Docile Lawyers: An Essay on the Pacification of Law Students' (1998) 111 *Harvard Law Review* 2027.

[19] Stuckey, above n. 11 at 22-23.

[20] MacCrate Report, above n. 11 at 236.

[21] Most American law schools also include legal research and writing in the first year curriculum. These courses typically focus exclusively on technical legal knowledge and skill (i.e., structure of courts, sources of law, citation and fundamentals of legal writing). The method of instruction in such skills courses, however, is sometimes used to reinforce a legal philosophy

expecting to examine the nature of law and justice in an academic environment will instead be overwhelmed by the repetitive briefing of cases to in order to develop the trade skills of the lawyer-plumber.[22]

In addition to the structure of the traditional first year experience, the traditional first year teaching method further isolates students from examining the philosophies underlying law. The traditional first year pedagogy is the Langdellian appellate case method combined with Socratic dialogue in the classroom.[23] The case method is useful and effective. The method develops the student's ability to critically deconstruct and examine case law (a skill essential to the formation of the lawyer's legal opinion and advice). The primary pedagogical purpose of the first year curriculum is development of the student's ability to think like a lawyer. The case method is well suited to this end. In an effort to develop rigorous analytical ability, first year professors usually use the Socratic teaching method merely to press the student to particular details of individual appellate decisions (i.e., what is this rule of this case).

But the case method is usually not effective at connecting the particular case to general principles of justice.[24] Accordingly, the student's desire to deepen their own understanding of justice is frustrated. This is an understatement. As will be explained below, the case method often ties the student in dialectic knots causing frustration leading to resignation that there must be no right answers to any question. This common experience results in the student's loss of interest in the pursuit of justice. Without the benefit of a preliminary examination of legal philosophy, first year students repeatedly dissect cases, describe the guts and learn the rules. Without the contextualization which would result from an contemporaneous examination of legal philosophy and allow the connection of the particular with the general, students and are left with the false impression that the law is nothing more than what is contained in the few appellate

which rejects the possibility of just answers to legal questions. *See eg* Julie M. Spanbauer, 'Teaching First-Semester Students that Objective Analysis Persuades' (1999) 5 *Legal Writing: The Journal of the Legal Writing Institute* 167, 170-71 (describing legal writing teaching techniques resting on the philosophic rejection of objectivity).

[22] *See* Erwin N. Griswold, 'Intellect and Spirit' (1967) 81 *Harvard Law Review* 292, 297.

[23] *See* Stuckey, above n. 11 at 207.

[24] I recognize that the case method and Socratic dialogue easily accommodate pursuit of first principles. However, because the primary goal of the first year is the development of analytical ability rather than the development of a solid jurisprudential foundation, the case method is often not used for development of the student's understanding of legal philosophy. Many professors use the method only to test the student's care in reading and deconstructing the particular case under examination. This practice is so prevalent in the American legal academy that there exists an industry devoted to the development of canned case briefs to guide the student through the Professor's Socratic questions.

opinions they encounter through the semester.[25] The traditional first year curriculum and pedagogy tosses students into the sea of common law and requires them to try and keep their heads above water. While they think they are drowning and are disoriented, many will stop asking "what is just?" and instead, looking for a plank floating in the water, only ask "what is the rule?"

Erwin Griswold, while he was Dean of Harvard Law School, noted both the utility and danger of the traditional first year teaching method:

> The case method is a powerful device for inculcating a certain type of logical reasoning. Experience with this type of reasoning is an essential part of legal education, for it is widely used by judges, lawyers, and laymen in dealing with legal problems. Thus, in this part of our work, the case method has great utility, particularly in exposing the shallow or inadequately supported reasoning to which many people are prone. In dealing with concrete situations, whether based on cases or on problems, it avoids the danger of too broad generalizations and teaches the student to be extremely careful of his own thinking and skeptical of the easy conclusions of others. But the case method alone does little more than this. It is only a tool. It is not an end in itself, and it is fully as dangerous as it is useful. A knife may be an instrument of mercy in the hands of a surgeon and a lethal weapon when used by another. So too, traditional methods of law school instruction may be dangerous and destructive in their results when used without adequate understanding; and this may be no less disastrous because it is wholly unintended.[26]

I agree with Dean Griswold's analysis. The case method is valuable and should not be eliminated from legal education. However, it is not enough, especially in the first year.

The following description of the typical student's experience in the first year will demonstrate the need for something more in the first year. The

---

25 Others have noted the tendency of the first year teaching method to have this effect. Alan Watson, for example, has argued that American casebooks should be replaced with "an amalgam of the standard British legal textbook and the American casebook. Each section of the book would contain an overview of the subject with citation of the important cases supporting each proposition. Then would come the presentation of the individual case with questions designed to improve students' analytical skills, and to show how and where the case fits in the overall context of the law. Teachers would both explain issues in the overview and test student skill in case analysis." *Legal Education Reform: Modest Suggestions*, 51 J. Legal Educ. 91 (2001).

26 Griswold, above n. 22 at 298-99.

case method and its intense focus on the process of legal reasoning conjoined with the repetitive search for individual rules of black letter law in each of the first year doctrinal courses fractures the law student's moral identity and results in a professional cynicism that will haunt the student in a profession committed to the pursuit of justice. Has this unbalanced first year curriculum and pedagogy sharpened minds at the expense the lawyer's ability to exercise judgment between that which is good and that which is not?[27]

In order to understand the impact of the first year it is important to consider the identity of the average matriculating student. One hundred years ago, when the traditional first year curriculum and case method were coalescing, law student populations were much less diverse than they are today.[28] Additionally, students entering law school one hundred years ago were much more likely than those matriculating today to have enjoyed a rigorous liberal arts undergraduate training. These factors are important for two reasons.

First, the traditional first year curriculum was developed with the presupposition that first year law students had already studied moral and political philosophy in their liberal arts education. Thus, many of the students entering law school had already examined the nature of justice as they read Plato, Aristotle, Cicero, Augustine, Aquinas, Kant, Bentham, Locke, Mill, Hobbes and others in pursuit of their undergraduate degrees. These students entered law school with some appreciation of the political and moral context of the law. The purposeful exclusion of legal philosophy from the first year, in this context, in pursuit of narrow analytical ability was unlikely to lead students to the conclusion that there is no such thing as justice. The entering law student's undergraduate education served as bedrock for the acquisition of the deconstructing power of the legal method.[29]

---

[27] Ibid. 'It has often been said, for a smile, that legal education sharpens the mind by narrowing it. To my mind, there is more truth to this than we have been willing to admit. The methods of legal education fostered at this school and widely adopted elsewhere do have a tendency to exalt dialectical skill, to focus the mind on narrow issues, and to obscure the fact that no reasoning, however logical, can rise above the premises on which is it based.'

[28] *See id.* at 18-25.

[29] Note that the structure of this education path, a general liberal arts education followed by rigorous analytical training, resembles the model of professional training still used in England. Students there begin with a foundation in theory in pursuit of their foundational degree in jurisprudence. The general study then leads to development of analytical and technical skills necessary for the lawyer's service to her clients and the profession.

Students entering law school today are much less likely than those entering one hundred years ago to have carefully thought about the nature of justice. The decline of general liberal arts education is well-known corollary to the academy's trend toward specialization. Unfortunately, such specialization results in students entering graduate school without a solid foundation in more general and conceptual knowledge. Students entering law school with degrees in business, economic, sociology, psychology or even pre-law have likely never carefully examined the nature of justice. Many are expecting to do that in law school. Anyone expecting to examine the nature of justice in their first few weeks of law school is in for an unwelcome surprise. Law school greets students with an intense specialization of its own, an effort to inculcate the legal method and "tough-minded" analytical skill.[30] Today's first year students, unless they have examined political or moral philosophy in college, often complete their first year in law school with the false impression that justice is nothing more than the legal method.

Second, the increasing diversity of matriculating students undermines another assumption shared by those who formulated the traditional first year curriculum. As will be discussed in more detail below, the first year curriculum and teaching method intentionally challenges first year students to set aside his moral and ethical presuppositions in order to learn "the law." The professor can carefully lead the class through this process when the class shares common presuppositions. However, when the presuppositions are more diverse, reflecting greater diversity within the classroom, then it is much more likely that the professor will lead some students to unintended ethical confusion and moral frustration as they these students attempt to follow down the Socratic path. Because today's students do not share a common foundation in western political thought the professor's Socratic dialogue is unlikely to lead all students down the same path.

With these characteristics in mind, now consider the experience of the typical first year student. First year students usually begin their legal education in America by spending hundreds of dollars on a set of casebooks for use in their doctrinal courses. Students typically begin reading and briefing cases before their first day of class.

For their torts sections, many first year students are required to purchase Dean William Prosser's casebook.[31] Prosser's name is synonymous American tort law

[30] *See* Cramton, above n.13 at 250-51.

[31] William L. Prosser, *Handbook of the Law of Torts* (1st ed, 1941) 1.

and his text has been one of the most widely utilized casebooks in the academy. The book is so well associated with the American law school experience that it has obtained recognition in American popular culture.[32] Perhaps the first thing, then, which an American law student encounters regarding the law of tort is Prosser's familiar definition: "A tort is a civil wrong, other than a breach of contract, for which the law provides a remedy."[33] I suspect that if one were to ask the average American lawyer what a tort is she would reply by reciting what she remembers of Prosser's well-known definition.

What jurisprudential conclusions might a first year student glean from Prosser's taxonomy of tort? Prosser's taxonomy is strikingly functional. He defines tort by referring to the availability of a remedy (a tort exist whenever "the law" provides a remedy). Prosser 's definition thereby avoids the difficult normative task of identifying principles useful for delineating wrongful conduct.[34] The neophyte is gently led to the realist's conception of justice, that a "wrong" is anything a court says it is nothing more.[35] Because the student is not enrolled in jurisprudence, a course in which the realist's conception of justice would be articulated and examined alongside other general theories of justice, the student presumes that Prosser's definition is correct and eagerly moves on to the examination of the first tort. A small seed of cynicism has already been planted in the student's mind via Prosser's taxonomy of tort.

As the student moves forward, they quickly encounter liability for intentional torts. Like many casebooks, Prosser's text introduces the student to the concept of intent with a series of cases before the moving into the first intentional tort. Many students, like others not yet reprogrammed by legal education, suspect that intentional conduct is any action chosen by the actor with the subjective purpose of accomplishing a particular result. Most students presume that one *intends* to inflict harm on another when one acts with the deliberate purpose of causing harm. The student's ethical instincts typically recognize the value of admonitory and regulatory functions of tort law. Students are, therefore,

---

[32] See Christopher J. Robinette, Prosser on Torts in Pop Culture (2009) <http://lawprofessors.typepad.com/tortsprof/2009/04/prosser-on-torts-in-pop-culture.html> at 29 August 2009.

[33] As has been noted elsewhere, this sentence was the opening sentence of each of the four editions of Prosser's text published during his lifetime. *See* John C. P. Goldberg, 'Ten Half-Truths about Tort Law' (2008) 42 *Valparaiso Law Review* 1221, 1222.

[34] Holmes pursued such first principles of tort, contract and criminal law in *The Common Law*. Oliver Wendell Holmes, Jr., *The Common Law* (first published 1881).

[35] Prosser's functional definition of tort is consistent with his formulaic approach to tort. *See* G. Edward White, *Tort Law in America: An Intellectual History* (1980) 157.

comfortable with the imposition of liability whenever there is proof that one deliberately inflicts harm on another.

The first case in Prosser's casebook regarding intent is *Garratt v. Dailey.*[36] The case regards the conduct of five-year old Brian Dailey. Brian pulled a chair away from its location while Ruth Garratt was in the process of sitting down. Garratt sued Brian for battery. The trial court dismissed the case after determining that Brian acted without intending to harm Garratt. This conclusion of law confirms the average law student's ethical impulses regarding liability: one is a "wrongdoer" only if one acts intending to harm another.

The Washington Supreme Court reversed the trial court explaining that "the mere absence of any intent to injure the plaintiff or to play a prank on her or to embarrass her, or to commit an assault and battery on here would not absolve him from liability if in fact he [knew Garratt would attempt to sit down where the chair had been.]"[37] This finding does not significantly disturb most students because it is very far removed from their moral instincts. There is not a significant distance between imposition of liability on proof of deliberate intent to cause harm and the imposition of liability on proof of voluntary action chosen by the actor possessing actual knowledge that harmful results will result will result from the actor's conduct. The student's instincts regarding the moral boundaries of tort liability is preserved by the court in *Garratt* with these words: "Without such knowledge, there would be nothing wrongful about Brian's act in moving the chair and, there being no wrongful act, there would be no liability."[38] The court remanded the case with instructions to the trial court to determine whether Brian acted possessing a substantial certainty that Garratt would sit down after he moved the chair. So far so good.

The very next case in Prosser's book subtlety introduces the student to one of the critical jurisprudential questions underlying tort law: the question of subjective verses objective standards of fault. The case is *Spivey v. Battaglia.*[39] The case involves physical injuries resulting from an unsolicited hug. The injuries were unintended (in layman's and first year law student's terms). The actor did not possess knowledge that his hug would result in harm to the plaintiff. Yet, the Florida Supreme Court imposed liability, reasoning that "the intent with which such a tort liability as assault is concerned is not necessarily a

36 (1955) 279 P 2d 1091.
37 Ibid 1094.
38 Ibid.
39 (1972) 258 SE 2d 815.

hostile intent, or a desire to do harm. Where a reasonable man would believe that a particular result was *substantially certain* to follow, he will be held in the eyes of the law as though he intended it."[40]

The law student's ethical instincts are now put to the test. Upon what moral or ethical basis does a court justify the leap from liability for deliberate intent or subjective knowledge of certain unlawful consequences of voluntary action to imposition of liability on the basis of an *ex post* analysis of the objective reasonableness of the actor's conduct based on the surrounding circumstances? This question is a critical jurisprudential issue. Despite the complexity and importance of the question, in the current edition of Prosser's text, the student is alerted to the issue only by the following brief note: "For a discussion of the treatment of intent in English and American law, *see* Finnis, 'Intention in Tort Law' in Owen, Philosophical Foundations of Tort Law 229 (Clarendon Press 1995)."[41]

While I appreciate the editors' decision to include an indication that the issue is connected to legal philosophy, there is no indication of the existence of disagreement concerning the imposition of tort liability on the basis of an objective conception of intent. The brief note is not adequate. The overwhelming majority of first year torts students will not read the Finnis excerpt contained in Owen's book. The editors of the casebook surely appreciate this fact. Most students will presume that their ethical instincts were wrong, they might be disturbed by a rule imposing liability for intentional conduct without requiring proof of actual subjective intent, but will undoubtedly put the objective standard in their notes and move on to search for other "rules" of tort law.

This is an extremely important moment in the development of the student's professional identity. The student has encountered a problematic ethical issue. Rather than attempt to reconcile the proposed rule of tort law with a sound theory of justice, the student is essentially compelled by the editorial decisions of the casebook authors and the pace of the curricular course of study (the torts professor is unlikely to spend more than part of one class working through the implications of the *Spivey* opinion) to set their ethical qualms aside, learn the rule and move on.

---

[40] Ibid 816-17.

[41] Victor E. Schwartz, Kathryn Kelly and David F. Partlett, *Prosser, Wade and Schwartz's Torts: Cases and Materials*, (11th ed. 2005) 23 n. 3.

Because first year students are not enrolled in jurisprudence prior to or at the same time as they study tort law, they are unlikely to work through the implications of any of the difficult issues they will encounter. Nor will these students work through the moral and ethical implications of the problematic rules they encounter in contract, property, civil procedure or criminal law. Students simply learn to dissect cases to identify the "rule of law," ignore their moral or ethical concerns and move on to the next case.

I am not arguing that Dean Prosser or any of his prestigious colleagues who have contributed to his text intentionally attempted to manipulating students by foisting on them a one-sided view of this foundational jurisprudential question.[42] Instead, I am attempting to illustrate the moral and ethical dilemma first year students confront during their first few days in the typical torts class as they attempt to learn the law by reading their assignments and briefing their cases. Without the benefit of the context provided by a general examination of the nature of law, neophytes in the study of tort law might understandably presume that they are learning what the law is merely by memorizing individual rules from a few cases, even if those rules do not correlate to the student's moral instincts.

Well, perhaps the typical classroom experience will clear up their moral confusion. What happens in class? Most professors, especially those in traditional common law courses, are eager to engage law students in Socratic dialogue in order to challenge the students' presuppositions and ethical impulses. This is especially true in the study of tort law.

In his own thoughtful examination of the legal profession's identity crisis, Walter Bennett traces the roots of cynicism in his own professional life to his legal education, specifically to an experience in his first year study of tort. He writes:

> Early in the semester our reading assignment included *Beatty v. Central Iowa Railway*, a relatively short nineteenth-century case presenting the elements of negligence and reasonable care, and we had discussed the case exhaustively under my professor's tutelage for the better part of two class meetings. I recall my intellectual and emotional disorientation

[42] If justice permits an objective standard of liability then it is arguable that the editors are personally liable for harm resulting from editorial decisions made with an objective ex post substantial certainty that harm resulted from the failure to integrate a more detailed and systematic discussion of the jurisprudential implications of adopting an objective standard of fault.

> in those first law school classes and the eagerness with which most of us sought direction in the jungle of questions that our teacher planted around us. I recall the cacophony of ideas, viewpoints, and voices our professor used to lead us about in that jungle and my feelings of being lost and bewildered when one attempt at closure after another was exposed as a false trail. . . . Finally, at a point well into the third class period when I was bound limb-for-limb in the dialectical tangle and feeling the hot breath of the leopard, one of my more vocal classmates (he actually volunteered answers – or, attempted answers) lunged for daylight. His attempted breakout came in his response to the last in a series of increasingly pointed questions from our professor about how reasoned analysis of the case could have led to the result my classmate had just proposed. At last cornered and growing desperate, my classmate blurted out: "Because it seems to be the best way to achieve justice." The professor, who was pacing by this time, whirled in his tracks, thrust both hands in the air and shouted in a voice louder than any I had heard indoors, "Don't speak to me of Justice! I do not wish to hear about Justice. I wish to hear about the rule of law." . . . I had assumed, as had the student who uttered the fatal words on justice, that justice was the whole point of law and the reason I was in law school. But no – not only was it not the point, it was not even in the equation. I had entered a system where such concepts were apparently viewed as worthless or worse, a hindrance to my success in the system.[43]

I include this lengthy passage for two reasons: (1) this passage reflects an experience shared by many who survived the first year; and (2) readers who have not been trained in an American law school may not be aware of the degree of antagonism there is in many first year classrooms to idealistic ethical and moral notions. Students who recognize the moral and ethical implications of various rules encountered in a typical first year torts course are often compelled to set those concerns aside and just learn the rules. Their desire to

[43] Walter Bennett, *The Lawyer's Myth* (2001) 13-14. Similar experiences are recorded in Benjamin Sell's *The Soul of the Law* 36 (1994). Professor Harold Berman, writing in 2001, recalls a similar experience occurring at the end of his education at Yale in the 1940s:

I recall vividly my last law-school class – it was in June 1947 (I had returned to law school after military service overseas) – when Professor Eugene Rostow, in the course in corporate finance, somehow brought the discussion around to the day's news of the failure of a South Carolina grand jury to indict persons charged with carrying out the lynching of a black man, though the evidence against them was overwhelming. "Is that justice?" Professor Rostow asked. "What *is* justice?" I remember it particularly because it was the first time the word *justice* had been mentioned in any of the courses I had taken during three years of law study.

Harold J. Berman, 'Forward' in Michael W. McConnell, Robert F. Cochran, Jr. and Angela C. Carmella (eds), *Christian Perspectives on Legal Thought* (2001) xi-xii.

reconcile ethical dilemmas posited by numerous rules encountered in the study of tort (i.e., liability without fault, objective standards of fault, contingency fees, etc.) is the natural reaction of moral beings to such questions as those being are engaged in the active pursuit of justice. But many professors, especially torts professors, consider this desire to be a distraction which must be eliminated if the legal method will work.

Every torts student in America is quickly exposed to the caveat that there is a great chasm separating moral and legal rules. Many judicial opinions included in first year casebooks drive a wedge between moral and legal language. Without opportunity for meaningful reflection or discussion, law students, like Walter Bennett's colleague, are warned against "confusing law and morality." Students often interpret these warnings as signposts pointing down a path leading to the conclusion that law is amoral.

American law professors have justified efforts to push their students' moral impulses out of the classroom by citing Justice Holmes' admonition in *The Path of Law* that there are "many evil effects of the confusion between legal and moral ideas."[44] Undoubtedly, Bennett's torts professor thought he was faithfully inculcating Holmsian analytical skill and pursuing Holmes' call for precision in legal reasoning. Such reasoning, said Holmes, resulted only "when we wash [moral terms] with cynical acid and expel everything except the object of our study."[45] The object of our legal education, as any realist will tell you, was well defined by Holmes: "When we study law we are not studying a mystery but a well known profession. . . . The object of our study, then, is prediction of the incidence of the public force through the instrumentality of the courts."[46]

As I will discuss below, there is an important and valuable pedagogical purpose in challenging the student to attempt to step outside of their own moral instincts in order to describe the law. In Holmes words, the student's instincts are often "fuzzy" and distract the student from the skill of predicting what a court will declare the law to be. More will be said regarding this valuable process below. For now I note that there is an important distinction between challenging a student to temporarily suspend their own moral instincts and demanding that the student to throw their moral identity out of the classroom permanently for the purpose of studying law. The professor's effort to cast all

[44] Oliver Wendell Holmes, Jr., 'The Path of the Law' (1897) 10 *Harvard Law Review* 457, 457-58.
[45] Ibid.
[46] Ibid.

moral questions out of the classroom, the attempt discuss the law only as it is rather than as it ought to be, fractures the law student's moral identity and sets the student up for much professional confusion and frustration.[47]

The first year experience is transformative. The student's analytical capacity increases but the student's thinking is in many ways now more limited. The skepticism developed by the first year legal method now compels the student to questions everything, including her own moral and ethical impulses. Without the assistance of legal, moral or political philosophy, the student who survives her first year is now thinking like a lawyer and heading toward the mental, emotional, physical and spiritual confusion plaguing many of her colleagues in the profession today. Is this the career path in the law Holmes intended? A closer examination of Holmes influential lecture reveals that the academy has, unfortunately, only heard half of what he had to say regarding learning the law. Our students would be well served if we would listen to everything that he was advocating instead of picking only those parts that advance our own skepticism.

II. Reconsidering the *Path of the Law*

On January 8, 1897, Oliver Wendell Holmes spoke at a ceremony at Boston University School of Law delivering an address to a group of lawyers, law professors and law students entitled *The Path of the Law.* His remarks, subsequently published in the Harvard Law Review,[48] have been read and cited by thousands of lawyers, law professors and law students since that day. To say that Holmes' lecture has been influential is a tremendous understatement.[49] Robert George has credited Holmes' lecture as the source of twentieth century legal philosophy.[50] The lecture is especially important to members of the legal academy because in it Holmes attempts to articulate a method of effectively studying law.

---

[47] Roger Cramton describes this harmful profession as follows:

Modern dogmas entangle legal education – a moral relativism tending toward nihilism, a pragmatism tending toward an amoral instrumentalism, a realism tending toward cynicism, an individualism tending toward atomism, and a faith in reason and democratic processes tending toward mere credulity and idolatry. We will neither understand nor transform these modern dogmas unless we abandon our unconcern for value premises. The beliefs and attitudes that anchor our lives must be examined and revealed.

Cramton, above n. 13 at 262.

[48] Holmes, above n. 44.

[49] "*The Path of the Law* is one of the great classics of the legal canon. Like so many classics, it endures because it is a catalyst for new ideas." Robert G. Bone, 'Forward: Symposium – The Path of the Law Today' (1998) 78 *Boston University Law Review* 691.

[50] Robert P. George, 'One Hundred Years of Legal Philosophy' (1999) 74 *Notre Dame Law Review* 1533.

Holmes begins: "When we study law we are not studying a mystery but a well known profession."[51] Holmes directs his audience away from the conceptualism prevalent during his generation, a search for axioms and formulas of law, to what he describes as the "true object of our study," an examination of an internal process of prediction, a method enabling lawyers to predict for their clients the likelihood of the "incidence of the public force through the instrumentality of the courts."[52]

Holmes' opening words, set in the place and time where they were spoken, were provocative. Formal legal education of Holmes' day was often conceptual and general rather than scientific and particular. In order to appreciate the context in which Holmes spoke, consider the reaction to Dean Langdell's introduction of the scientific case method at Harvard just thirty years earlier. Certain members of the Harvard faculty were so upset by Dean Langdell's effort to divorce the study of law from the examination of general principles to the study of individual appellate decisions that they resigned from Harvard and founded the law school at Boston University.[53]

Holmes' words to the audience at Boston University seemed to demand a movement away from pursuing general principles and universal truths to conceiving the study of law as an entirely internal examination of the legal process used to predict the instrumental use of public power. This interpretation of Holmes' words is bolstered by his assertion that the "confusion between legal and moral ideas" within legal education was the cause of "many evil effects."[54] According to Holmes, legal education should direct the student to the "narrow path of legal doctrine" by banishing "every word of moral significance altogether, and other words adopted which should convey legal ideas uncolored by anything outside the law."[55]

With these statements the American legal realism movement was conceived. Importantly, the legal realism movement Holmes fathered took shape during the same period of time when the traditional first year curriculum was falling into place in the American legal academy. The realists, citing Holmes, began demanding a strict separation in law school classrooms between law and morality. According to Dean Cramton, the realists were successful in achieving

---

51 Holmes, above n. 44 at 457.

52 Ibid.

53 "Even from the moment of its introduction, Langdell's case method was the subject of controversy. Members of the faculty withdrew from the school. It is recorded in the *Centennial History of the Harvard Law School* that 'as a protest against' the case method, 'the Law School of Boston University was founded, having on its faculty eminent members of the Boston bar, and for many years it was regarded as a more practical school for lawyers than the Harvard Law School." Griswold, above n. 22 at 294-95.

54 Holmes, above n. 44 at 458.

55 Ibid.

this separation: "one of the most insistent notions [frequently encountered in legal education] is that there is an unbridgeable chasm between 'facts' (which are 'real' or 'hard' or 'tangible') and 'values' (which are 'subjective' or 'soft' or 'intangible'). The distinction between the *is* and the *ought*, the legal realists said, was temporary and was designed merely to free legal scholars so they could take a fresh and critical look at how officials actually behaved, all as a preliminary to the main task of reforming legal institutions in the light of the suspended goals."[56] Similarly, the suspension of the law student's own instincts regarding what the law ought to be, realists would argue, is necessary to develop the student's ability to predict and describe what law actually is.

Walter Bennett's experience in his torts class is illustrative of the process. The torts professor led the student down a familiar Socratic path with the knowledge that the student's moral and ethical desire to achieve justice would conflict with what the rule announced in the case actually was. Rather than guiding the student through the difficult process of reconciling the student's instincts regarding what the law ought to be with the rule of law announced in the case under review, the professor threw the discussion of what ought to be out of the classroom. Bennett acknowledges, and I agree, that there was pedagogical value in this process: "[The torts professor] was admonishing [his students] to forget (at least temporarily) the fuzzier notions of justice and morality in order to learn the rigorous process of legal analysis – to learn, as [] Holmes put it, 'to predict the incidence of public force through the instruments of the courts.'"[57] But Bennett has correctly identified a critical pedagogical failure in his professor's approach, a failure which I argue fractures the moral identity of the typical first year student: "the problem is that no one told me and my classmates that the separation of law from morality was temporary. Indeed, the entire attitude of the law school hierarchy, both in the law school I attended and in many others then and now, is that man's highest achievement is rigorous legal analysis and that serious students of the law must pay primary, in not exclusive, fealty to that purpose. Notions of justice and a higher morality are treated as distractions."[58]

This pedagogy remains central to the first year of legal education in American law schools. The inculcation of Holmsian analytic skill has become what Dean Cramton referred to as the "ordinary religion of the law school classroom."[59] According to Cramton, the religion inculcated in the American law school classroom consists of the following core tenants: "a skeptical attitude toward generalizations; an instrumental approach to law and lawyering; a 'tough-

[56] Cramton, above n. 13 at 254.

[57] Bennett, above n. 38 at 16.

[58] Ibid.

[59] Cramton, above n.13.

minded' and analytical attitude toward legal tasks and professional roles; and a faith that man, by the application of his reason and the use of democratic processes, can make the world a better place."[60] The neophyte is accepted into the system when he develops the lawyer's ability to insure that "affirmations of value (our desires concerning what ought to be) do not intrude upon thought and knowledge and fact concerning what *is*."[61] This initiation is usually complete by the end of the first year. The student will never think (or feel?) the way they did before they were converted.

Arguably, the environment within the average American law school classroom has become less orthodox since Cramton's time. However, many of the factors identified by Cramton which inhibit the moral development of law students remain embedded in law schools, especially within the traditional first year curriculum and pedagogy. These factors include: a steady diet of borderline cases (what Dworkin calls "hard cases"); the opaqueness and arbitrariness of line-drawing in such hard cases; an overemphasis on uncertainty and instability of law; a tendency to teach students to advocate legal positions in light of the existing law rather than development of ability to articulate proper ends; the failure to discuss the lawyer's role in law creation; and an explicit avoidance of value discussions in the classroom.[62] Based on the research of Professor Bennett, many of these factors appear to remain part of the law school classroom and continue to cause law students to experience "moral alienation" as a result of the teaching method.[63]

Is this the educational experience Holmes was advocating? No. Holmes advocated pursuit of what he described as a "great life in the law." He also lived this life. I doubt whether he would approve of any pedagogy resulting in what Dean Anthony Kronman has described as the demise of the legal profession's soul.[64]

---

60 Ibid at 248.

61 Ibid.

62 Ibid. at 253-56.

63 Bennett, above n. 38 at 18. Professor Alan Watson surveyed members of an upper level seminar at the University of Georgia regarding their experiences in law school and published the results of his survey in the *Journal of Legal Education.* (2001) 51 *Journal of Legal Education* 91. These results provide additional support for the conclusion that students are frustrated by their first year experience. Watson writes: 'I was horrified that none of the students had anything good – not one thing – to say about legal education (though they did recognize that some professors were good teachers) . . . All said that the first year in law school was a horrible experience. More than one claimed that it was the worst year of their lives.': at 91. Watson's students also noted that ethical issues received inadequate treatment throughout law school.: at 92.

64 Kronman, above n. 7 at 1.

Holmes warned his audience against misinterpreting his words: "I take it for granted that no hearer of mine will misinterpret what I have to say as the language of cynicism. The law is the witness and external deposit of our moral life."[65] Holmes was not asserting that in the process of studying law students should become unmoored from their moral identities and divorced from their own ideals. Near the end of his lecture Holmes warns his audience against too much focus on the machinery of legal education. He notes that "theory is the most important part of the dogma of the law, as the architect is the most important man who takes part in building of a house."[66] It is hard to believe that the author of this statement would approve of a curriculum that focuses entirely on the machinery of doctrinal law at the expense of a careful study of legal philosophy.

There is no doubt that Holmes called for the law student's temporary suspension of moral reasoning for the limited purpose of studying the nature of the legal system as it is rather than as the student thinks it ought to be. But those who have excluded moral and legal philosophy from the first year law school curriculum, citing Holmes, have failed to consider his final admonition: "The remoter and more general aspects of the law are those which give it universal interest. It is through them that you not only become a great master in your calling, but connect your subject with the universe and catch an echo of the infinite, a glimpse of its unfathomable process, a hint of the universal law."[67] Holmes recognized that in order to master the lawyer's craft one must reconcile their determination of what is with what it ought to be. The academy's failure to join Holmes in acknowledging this truth (the insistence that there is nothing external to the positive law) has led to a crisis within legal education and the legal profession.

In Dean Cramton's words, the primary aim of all education "is to encourage a process of continuous self-learning that involves the mind, spirit and body of the whole person. This cannot be done unless larger questions of truth and meaning are directly faced. If all law and truth are relative, pressing our views on others would be arrogant and mischievous. But if there is really something that can be called truth, beauty or justice – even if in our finiteness we cannot always agree on what it is – then law school can be a place of searching and creativity that aspires to identify and accomplish justice . . . If truth and justice have no reality or coherence, what does a lawyer have to do?"[68] What is it we are training students to do?

---

65 Holmes, above n. 44 at 459.

66 Ibid at 477.

67 Ibid at 478.

68 Cramton, above n. 13 at 263.

An answer is found in the preamble to the model rules of professional conduct lawyers are officers of the legal system "having special responsibility for the quality of justice."[69] Is this a meaningless statement? Is the law student required to continue her suspension of moral reason as she enters the profession? If the answer to these questions is no, and surely the answer is no, then the legal academy should reconsider the exclusion of moral order from its first year classrooms. Law students should be given permission (and perhaps required) to pursue an understanding of what is just. The following section will outline a proposal for a modest reform of the traditional first year curriculum and first year pedagogy which will purposefully reintegrate the pursuit of justice with the study of law.

III. A Proposed Remedy: Connecting the Is and the Ought

Many have noted problems within the current structure, curriculum and pedagogy of the American law school. The Carnegie Report, MacCrate Report and Best Practices reports all encourage curricular reform in order to better prepare law students for entry into the profession.[70] These reports have received much attention within the American legal academy and have sparked a variety of curricular reforms.[71] Most schools implementing or considering curricular changes are focused on reshaping the second and third year.[72] As I have argued above, much of the damage to the student's professional identity is already completed before the second year. Accordingly, changes to the second and third years are inadequate to remedy the intense skepticism and the impulse to brush off challenging ethical issues embedded in the law student as a result of the traditional first year curriculum and pedagogy. Changes in the first year are necessary.

I am not suggesting that the traditional first year curriculum and pedagogy must be thrown out. The traditional first year program effectively develops and sharpens analytical ability fundamental to effective participation in the practice of law. The case method is effective because it replicates an analytical and argumentative process really used in practice. Students must develop proficiency in deconstructing case law, identifying relevant legal arguments and predicting what a court is likely to hold in a particular case. Holmes correctly noted that clients pay lawyers for a specific service, that of predicting whether

[69] American Bar Association, Center for Professional Responsibility, 'Preamble and Scope,' *Model Rules of Professional Conduct* (2007 ed.) 1.

[70] Above n. 11.

[71] A helpful summary of the curricular reforms under consideration or adopted in the American academy is available at <http://lawteaching.org/publications/ILTLchartoflegaleducationreform200905.pdf> at 29 August 2009.

[72] Ibid.

or not the client's proposed conduct violates the letter of the law. Thus, students should be trained to dispassionately evaluate whether or not the client's conduct will result in the "incidence of the public force through the instrumentality of the courts." [73] The repetition of case briefing together with Socratic dialogue is effective in imparting these fundamental skills and must not be eliminated from the first year experience.

Acknowledging that the case method has pedagogical value, however, does not mean that its use must be continued in every first year course. The great pedagogical weakness in the traditional first year curriculum is a consequence of an overly narrow conception of the *telos* of legal education. The structure, curriculum and pedagogy of most first year programs in the American legal academy have narrowly focused on one primary objective: the development of rigorous, dispassionate, analytical "tough mindedness." The sharpening of the first year student's mind has often come at the expense of the student's body and spirit. This unbalanced effort to sharpen minds, ironically, damages the student's intellect.[74] This problem cannot be remedied by altering the content of the second or third year (especially for those students on whom the sword of attrition falls. They leave law school with a very narrow and, most likely, negative view of law and the legal profession).

Consider education in a different context. Kindergarten students should be taught their alphabet because they will need the ability to work with their ABC's in the real world. But this does not mean that the ABC's are the only thing that these youngsters should study. We should also teach them how to count, paint and play. Similarly, neophyte lawyers should be taught skills fundamental to their trade but they need more than technical legal skill to flourish in their professional life. More can be accomplished in the first year of legal education than just sharpening minds. We can, by offering our students a broader view of

---

[73] Holmes, above n. 44 at 457.

[74] Dean Griswold noted his observation of this phenomena among the students he observed during his years at Harvard:

I would like to suggest that another consequence of the unthoughtful use of traditional approaches to legal instruction is the exaltation of rationality over other values which are of great importance to our society. Note that I said "rationality," and not intellectualism, for I am not making an anti-intellectual point. Quite the contrary. The very essence of my submission is that in exalting purely logical reasoning, sometimes almost of the chess or bridge game type, we are not giving sufficient weight to other elements in the situation which are equally relevant in any truly intellectual evaluation. We push and squeeze our students; we question them and prod them; we indicate our belief in the minutiae. Be again and again we stress logic as the ultimate objective, though we may be rather unaware that we are doing so. We encourage imagination – in small ways, and perhaps in analogical reasoning. But do we encourage imagination in the broad sense? Do we encourage our students to devise new premises, to start out on whole new lines of reasoning, to come up with new solutions?

Griswold, above n.22 at 300-01.

the nature of law and legal reasoning in their first semester, inspire our students to use their new analytical skills to pursue things which are beautiful and just. How would we do this? The first year should become a more balanced educational experience with the integration of a course during the first semester exposing the student to the nature of law and the lawyer's role in the legal system. I would call this course *Law, the Lawyer and Justice.* The course description would read as follows:

> *This course is a foundational course introducing the law student to the concept of law and to the legal profession. What is law? What is justice? This course will introduce different answers to these fundamental questions by examining various theories of justice prevalent in the western legal tradition including natural law and natural rights theory, positivism, utilitarianism, legal realism, critical legal studies and enlightenment liberalism. This course will also introduce the student to the structure of law and the lawyer's obligations within the legal system. This examination will introduce the student to the adversarial process and the lawyer's ethical obligations to the client, bench and bar.*

This course would give law students a solid foundation in legal philosophy on which to stand while they develop analytical skills critical to the lawyer's craft. As Alan Watson has said, we should purposefully cater to the need of both lawyer philosopher and lawyer plumber for both are necessary to a healthy profession and society.[75]

The first year reform I am suggesting begins with a careful reexamination of first year pedagogical objectives and desired outputs. This first step has been recommended by the Carnegie Foundation Report, the MacCrate Report and the Best Practices for Legal Education report. Each of these reports includes data and recommendations useful for development of more balanced first year teaching objectives.[76] Schools should consider what the current outputs of the traditional first year program. If the school is happy with the current output of the first year program then it may not pursue any reform.

---

[75] Watson, above n. 25 at 93.

[76] The MacCrate Report, for example, invites such use: "Law Schools can use the [Report] as a focus for examining proposals to modify their curricula to teach skills and values more extensively or differently than they do now. Such modifications might include, for example: revisions of conventional courses and teaching methods to more systematically integrate the study of skills and values with the study of substantive law and theory." MacCrate , above n. 11 at 128.

The traditional first year program, as demonstrated above, produces second year students who often lose sight of the forest for the trees. The case method, often used in all but their first year legal writing sections, has turned their minds away from contemplation of general concepts to the rigorous tough-minded focus on taxonomy which the case-method was designed to produce. The remedy is to expose students early in their legal education to the forest by adding legal philosophy into the first year as a foundational course alongside the traditional doctrinal courses. This change would satisfy the entering student's desire to study the nature of law and justice, counteract the tendency of the typical doctrinal course toward the atomistic and particular by exposing law students to general theories of justice and improve the student's understanding of the lawyer's role in society.

This change, I argue, would enhance the student's experience in the other traditional first year course by enabling the student to more carefully examine cases they are briefing in their other courses. For example, if law students were introduced to the law and economics movement in a legal philosophy course, the student's ability to understand and the premises underlying product liability theories in tort would be much improved. In my experience, it is difficult to pursue a careful analysis of the law and economics movement in torts because the primary pedagogical objective of the course (i.e., Socratic questioning designed to develop the student's analytical skills) leaves little time for anything else. Students acquire the ability to sense the theory floating behind the rule[77] but are forced to settle on learning the rule in order to move on to the next one. It is very difficult to counteract this tendency in doctrinal courses due to the pressure to cover all of the traditional black letter law. Classroom discussion in all of the doctrinal courses would be much improved if students had already been introduced to general legal theory in a foundational course.

Some will argue that addition of the course I propose will not remedy the problems identified above and that my proposal amounts to nothing more than "tinkering with the curriculum." I offer several responses to this criticism. First, I am not arguing that the addition of one course is the only or the complete remedy to the problems diagnosed above. Experiential learning, apprenticeship

---

[77] On other occasions the theory behind the rule is overt. For example, on the third day of my first semester section of torts this fall, the casebook assignment included *Mohr v. Williams*, (1906) 108 NW 2d 818. The *Mohr* court held that a battery occurred, despite the good faith and skillful and successful conduct of the surgeon, because the plaintiff had not consented to an operation on her right ear but not her left. The court rested its holding on the "natural right" of the plaintiff to autonomy. Thus, the students are exposed to a controversial premise of great importance but due to the pedagogical goals of the course I was unable to proceed to a discussion of natural law theory.

or other non-traditional methods of education might also be beneficial. For a variety of reasons, however, I doubt whether the addition of experiential learning or mandatory clinical experiences in the first year is a feasible or reasonable solution to the lack of balance within the first year curriculum. Second, tinkering with the curriculum is required when the problem is caused by curricular imbalance. As Professor Krieger has noted, it is important address the imbalance *within* the curriculum and not attempt to resolve this problem at orientation or by other extracurricular activity. Third, I am not proposing "just another class." The course I propose would pursue pedagogical objectives different from the traditional first year doctrinal course and expose students to a wider variety of reading materials regarding law. Rather than developing analytical skill, the course I propose would assist the student's development of professional identity.

A few law schools have departed from the traditional first year curriculum. St. Thomas School of Law, for example, has added a course titled *Foundations of Justice* to its first year curriculum. According to the course description, the course is intended to "implement a pervasive approach to integrating faith and reason in a search for truth with a focus on morality and social justice."[78] Regent Law School requires its first year students to enroll in a course entitled *Christian Foundations of Law* described as a jurisprudential survey of the Christian foundations of Anglo-American law.[79] The University of Detroit Mercy School of Law recently revised its first year curriculum and added a required course entitled *Core Concepts* intended to broaden the entering students understanding of the legal process and the relationship between theory and practice.[80]

---

78 See <http://www.stthomas.edu/law/academics/Courses/Foundations%20of%20Justi.html> at 29 August 2009. For a description of St. Thomas' first year program see <http://www.stthomas.edu/law/academics/Firstyear.html> at 29 August 2009.

79 *See <http://www.regent.edu/acad/schlaw/academics/req_courses.cfm>* at 29 August 2009. This course is described as follows: "Jurisprudential survey of the Christian foundations of Anglo-American law, including the development of higher/natural law thinking, higher law influence on the development of the common law, the rise of modern legal philosophies and the influence of Christian and secular worldviews on the development of American law."

80 *See <http://www.law.udmercy.edu/prospective/curriculum/index.phpI>* at 29 August 2009. The course is described as follows: "The Core Concepts course introduces students to a wide range of theoretical approaches and analytical techniques for approaching legal problems. Students then apply these theories and techniques to a set of problems that cut across torts, contracts, property, and civil procedure. This problem solving experience is a better way to teach students theory by having them apply it and to show them that most legal issues do not fit neatly within boxes labeled 'torts,' 'property,' 'contracts,' etc."

These new courses illustrate a renewed receptivity to consideration of the conceptual along with the empirical in legal education. It will likely be noted that each of these institutions is a religiously affiliated law school. Religiously affiliated schools are surely not the only institutions concerned about the issues discussed in this essay. It is my presumption that all law schools are concerned about the health and wholeness of students. However, many religiously affiliated institutions, like the one at which I teach, pursue missions unlike traditional law schools in an important way: our institutions affirm the existence of ideals, norms and values external to human law. My faith tradition, for example, affirms that God is and that this God is the author of justice who has demonstrated his justice, mercy and love through the life, death and resurrection of Jesus Christ.[81] This affirmation, undoubtedly, impacts the pedagogy, legal philosophy and professional identity of those within my faith tradition who now call Christ Lord. But this affirmation does not lead to a single, narrow, close-minded, anti-intellectual view of the world. Christianity has contributed much to the development of western law and still has much to offer.[82]

One attribute common in many religiously affiliated schools is the belief that education of students requires demands more than sharpening minds. My institution's mission statement, for example, expresses our desire to "glorify God through education of the whole person, emphasizing integrity of character in a caring Christian environment where every individual matters every day."[83] Pepperdine University's affirmation of faith provides another illustration: 'Pepperdine University affirms . . . That the educational process may not, with impunity, be divorced from the divine process; That the student, as a person of

---

[81] Faulkner University is affiliated with the churches of Christ. For a description of Faulkner's mission *see* <http://www.faulkner.edu/discover/ataglance.asp> at 29 August 2009. Pepperdine University is also affiliated with the churches of Christ and its affirmation of faith is available at <http://seaver.pepperdine.edu/about/mission/affirmation.htm> at 29 August 2009.

[82] *See eg* McConnell, above n. 43. This book contains essays contributed by more than two dozen legal scholars illustrating a variety of legal perspectives claiming a connection to the Christian tradition. In his forward to the book, Professor Berman explains that the essays in the book are united less by theology than by their shared philosophic inquiry. He identifies two questions of moral philosophy unifying the project:

[O]ne is the analysis of law in general, and of various branches of the law, from the perspective of Christian concepts of justice and injustice; the other is the critique of major contemporary schools of legal thought which, in the guise of pragmatism, reflect (in the words of Albert W. Alschuler) 'the vices of atomism, alienation, ambivalence, self-centeredness, and vacuity of commitment that are characteristic of our culture.' One can hear in this an echo of Jesus' reprimand, 'Woe unto you lawyers, for you tithe mint and dill and cumin but neglect the weightier matters of the law, which are justice and mercy and good faith.' (Matthew 23:23).

Berman, above n.38 at xiii.

[83] Above n. 81.

infinite dignity, is the heart of the educational enterprise . . . That truth, having nothing to fear from investigation, must be pursued relentlessly in every discipline.'[84] These mission statements reflect what Christ identified as the first command: 'Love the Lord your God with all your heart and with all your soul and with all your strength and with all your mind.'[85] This integrated view of education also reflects an emerging post post-modern coherentist epistemology. Albert Alschuler describes this epistemology as one portraying "analogy, induction and deduction as a single continuous process."[86] These views of human reason encourage the integrated pursuit of technical legal skill along with a deeper understanding of the moral and legal philosophy underlying the legal process.

The most recent edition of the American Association for Law School's *Journal of Legal Education* includes a symposium regarding the role of religiously affiliated law schools in the legal academy.[87] As a faculty member at a religiously affiliated law school, it is my belief that institutions which affirm the existence of ideals, norms and values external to the law will contribute to the health of the legal academy and profession. At the very least, scholars at religiously affiliated institutions will sharpen the arguments of those rejecting external norms by critiquing the premises underlying competing conceptions of law and justice.

But even more than this, religiously affiliated law schools overtly recognize what is true of all law schools, the fact that all law schools confront values and belief. Dean Cramton rightly explains that "law schools and legal educators are inevitably involved in the service of values. For the most part they serve as priests of the established order and its modern dogmas. The educator has an obligation to address the values that he is serving; and there is room for at least a few prophets to call the legal profession and the larger society back to a covenant faith and moral commitment that it has forsaken."[88] The great fallacy of the realists (who were largely responsible for the formation of the traditional first year curriculum) is their claim that it is possible to step outside of one's own moral identity, spit out legal predictions like a machine without ever needing to reconcile the answers with values external to the legal machine. The realists claimed to possess no legal philosophy – but, in fact, inculcated a legal

---

84 Ibid.

85 Luke 10:27 (NIV).

86 'A Century of Skepticism' in McConnell, above n. 43 at 101.

87 John Garvey, 'AALS Symposium on Institutional Pluralism: The Role of Religiously Affiliated Law Schools' (2009) 59 *Journal of Legal Education* 1, 125.

88 Cramton, above n.13 at 263.

philosophy now reflected in the doubt, skepticism and valueless values commonly shared by members of the ailing American legal profession.[89] The current condition of the legal profession is a consequence of the failure of the realists to allow law students of generations past to imagine the possibility of what the condition of the profession otherwise might have been, trapping lawyers in the real world instead of upholding the possibility of the world as it ought to be.

[89] Dean Prosser, for example, claimed that he had no legal philosophy. William Prosser, 'My Philosophy of Law' (1942) 27 *Cornell Law Quarterly* 292, 295.

SOVEREIGNTY-ITS CONCOMITANT INGREDIENTS, ITS PRAGMATIC CONSTRAINTS AND ISLAMIC JURISPRUDENCE: A CRITICAL APPRAISAL

Dr. Nehaluddin A.[Δ]
Multimedia University Of Malaysia

Abstract: The modern concept of sovereignty has had many implications and many writers have tried to deal with them in their own way according to the circumstances in which they lived and, moreover, according to the problems they wanted to address through it.

In the wake of new developments and globalisation, which is associated not only with a new 'sovereignty regime' but also with the emergence of powerful new non-territorial forms of economic and political organisation in the global domain. Globalisation in this account is, therefore, associated with a transformation an unbundling of relationship between sovereignty, territoriality and state power. The traditional conceptualisation of sovereignty was simply a transitional phase in the legal philosophy and whether thoughts of Hobbes and Austin regarding sovereignty can no longer hold feasible in our contemporary world?

The paper will try to examine the concept of 'Sovereignty', the state power and territoriality thus stand today in a more complex relation than in the epoch during which the modern nation-states were forged in the post- world war era. It will also focus on Islamic viewpoint of sovereignty; we mean the whole range of those attributes which are imperative to dominate human intelligence and rationality while laying down the guidelines for the governance.

INTRODUCTION

The modern definition of sovereignty is generally attributed to John Austin. No doubt, he was the first jurist who articulated its concept in such a manner that well suited the legal structure of England. Though written with the

Δ MA, LLB, LLM. (Luck. India) LLM. (Strathclyde, UK), LLD. (India), Principal Lecturer, Faculty of Business and Law, Multimedia University, Jalan Ayer Keroh Lama, 75450 Melaka Malaysia. E-mail: ahmadnehal@yahoo.com Mobile No: +60166054353

predominant consideration of British legal system, yet the phraseology which Austin used to define the term 'sovereign' and 'sovereignty' still remains a juristic reality despite all the criticisms from various quarters.

'Sovereignty' - The theory of sovereignty which Austin adopts from Hobbes' political philosophy and, to a lesser extent, from Bentham's commentaries on Blackstone is intended to serve these purposes.[1]

What makes commands rules is the element of generality in them; what makes rules Laws- in the sense of positive laws, the subject of Austin's jurisprudence - is the fact that they are direct or indirect commands of the sovereign of an independent political society .These commands are addressed to the members of that society, who are thus subjects of that sovereign.

It is essential to note that he always means by sovereign the office or institution which embodies supreme authority; never the individuals who happen to hold that office or embody that institution through their relationships at any given time. Austin's sovereign is an abstraction —the location of the ultimate power which allows the creation of law in a society. As will appear later, this point is of the greatest importance, since he has often been criticised for describing sovereignty and the source of legal authority in 'personal' terms. Undoubtedly he felt no need to labour the matter for, in the tradition of political theory which he relies on; sovereignty is explicitly 'abstract'. Hobbes writing in the context of Cromwellian England, describes sovereignty as the 'artificial soul' of 'an artificial man', the latter being the state or commonwealth. The sovereign is an office not a particular person or particular people.[2]

Though generally credited with being the pioneer in the field, John Austin can simply be considered as the jurist who developed the notion of 'sovereignty', the raw material for which had already been supplied by Jeremy Bentham and prior to him by Hobbes. Making a comparison between Bentham and Austin on this point, Joseph Raz observes;

"Sovereignty"–Bentham, 'When a number of persons', he wrote, '(whom we may style subjects) are supposed to be in the habit of paying obedience to a person or an assemblage of persons, of a known and certain description (whom

[1] Roger Cotterrell, *The Politics of Jurisprudence — A Critical Introduction to Legal Philosophy* 1989, (Butterworths, London and Edinburgh), 67.
[2] Ibid 67-68.

we may call governor and governors) such persons together (subjects and governors) are said to be in a state of political society.'

One need only compare this passage with the following from the Province, p.194 to realize how great Austin's debt to his master is. If a determinate human superior, not in the habit of obedience to a like superior, receives habitual obedience from the bulk of a given society , that determinate superior is sovereign in that society, and the society (including the superior) is a society political and independent .[3]

A vague idea had already been given by Hobbes, What is the sovereign of an independent political society? Hobbes had defined such a society as one which could defend itself, unaided, against any attack from without.[4]

Yet Austin, more than any other writer, provided the compact and systematic formulation of a conception of law which allowed an escape from the tradition-bound theory implicit in classical common law thought.[5]

SOME BASIC CHARACTERISTICS OF SOVEREIGN

Describing the basic characteristics of sovereign as enunciated by John Austin, Roger Cotterrell says;

'Some characteristics of Austin's sovereign: It must be common (that is only one sovereign can exist in any political society; the sovereign is, in that sense, indivisible although it can be made up of several components) that it must be determinate (that is, the composition of the sovereign body or the identity of the sovereign person must be clear). A further characteristic has produced more controversy than any other aspect of Austin's conception of sovereignty .That is that the sovereign is illimitable by law. This follows directly from Austin's definition of law. Every law is the direct or indirect command of the sovereign of an independent political society.'[6]

Austin provided what historical jurisprudence could not; a clear designation of the scope of legal knowledge, an orderly theory of law which allowed the legal to be distinguished from the non-legal and the logical connections between

[3] Joseph Raz , *The Concept Of a legal System - An Introduction to The Theory of Legal System*, Second Edition- 1980 (Clarendon Press –Oxford), 6.
[4] Roger Cotterrell , above n 1, 68
[5] Ibid 52.
[6] Ibid 69.

legal ideas to be made explicit. Finally he offered a way of looking at law which made legislation central rather than peripheral .Thus his legal theory recognized the reality of the modern state as a massive organization of power.[7]

One of Austin's most important successors (Hart, 1955) goes on to remark that 'within a few years of his death it was clear that his work had established the study of jurisprudence in England'. (Austin died in 1859)[8]

The basic ingredients of Austinian concept of 'sovereign' and 'sovereignty', according to Joseph Raz,
'Existence criterion - A law is a general command of a sovereign to his subjects. In contrast to Bentham (and Kelsen) Austin thinks that only general commands, i.e. those obliging to acts or forbearances of a class', are laws.'[9]

For Austin a command is defined in terms of the following six conditions: C is A's command if and only if(1) A desires some other persons to behave in a certain way (2) he has expressed this desire (3) he intends to cause harm or pain to these persons if his desire is not fulfilled; (4) he has some power to do so (5) he has expressed his intention to do so and finally (6) C expresses the content of his desire and of his intention and nothing else .In Austin's own words;
'.......But a command is distinguished from other significations of desire by this peculiarity; that the party to whom it is directed is liable to evil from the other, in case he comply not with the desire. (Province, p.14 and p.17)'[10]

A law is part of a legal system if and only if it was enacted directly or indirectly by the sovereign of that system (Austin), or if and only if it is authorized by the basic norm of the system (Kelsen), or if and only if it ought to be recognized according to the rule of recognition of the system (Hart).These three philosophers were not concerned with the material unity of legal systems.[11]

'Austin says that sovereignty is the power of affecting others with evil or pain and of enforcing them, through fear of that evil, or fashion their conduct to one's wishes'. (Province, 24)[12]

---

[7] Ibid 69.
[8] Ibid 52.
[9] Joseph Raz , above n 3, 11.
[10] Ibid 11.
[11] Joseph Raz , *The Authority of Law — Essays on law and Morality*, 1979,(Clarendon Press – Oxford), 79.
[12] Josef Raz ,above n 3,12-3

Where there is the smallest chance of incurring the smallest evil, the expression of a wish amounts to a command and, therefore, imposes a duty.[13] 'Any particular law may be disregarded and constantly violated, and still exist, so long as the legal system of which it is a part is on the whole obeyed.'[14]

THE PRAGMATIC CONSTRAINTS OF SOVEREIGNTY

Hobbes, Bentham, Austin and others who followed them in advocating the institution of sovereign having absolute powers within a given society might have been prompted by the political set-up of their own times. They perhaps wanted to discourage any effective challenge to the unbridled authority of the person or persons that happened to be at the helm of affairs and thus to strengthen the existing institutions.

The sovereign state thus emerges to vindicate the supremacy of the secular order against religious claims; and it forces the clerics into the position of subordinate authority from which, after the Dark Ages, it had itself so painfully emerged .It is argued by Bodin, as later by Hobbes in a period of similar disintegration, that if the state is to live there must be in every organised political community some definite authority not only itself obeyed ,but also itself beyond the reach of authority. This was the root of Hobbes' argument .The will of the state must be all or nothing. If it can be challenged the prospect of anarchy is obvious. … A sovereign people, they argued cannot suffer derogation from the effective power of their instruments. Its will must be unimpeachable if it is to direct the destinies with which it is charged .We must not forget the atmosphere, not merely in which the theory of sovereignty was born, but also in which, at the hands of each of its great exponents ,it has secured new emphasis. That has been always, from Bodin to Hegel, a period of crisis in which the state seemed likely to perish unless it could secure the unified allegiance from its members.[15]

Laski elaborates,
'Those who have most powerfully shaped the theory of sovereignty — Bodin, Hobbes, Rousseau, Bentham and Austin — were, with the exception of Austin, all of them writing before the nature of federal state had been at all fully explored Either, like Bodin, they thought in terms of unlimited power of the

[13] Ibid 13.
[14] Ibid 16.

[15] Harold J.Laski , *A Grammar Of Politics*, First published in 1925,1982,(George Allen and Unwin Publishers Ltd.), 46.

prince, or, like Bentham, in terms of the unlimited power of the legislature; and they might, like Rousseau, deny legitimacy to any act which emanated merely from a representative organ.'[16]

Bodin developed one of the most celebrated definitions of sovereignty. Sovereignty, in this account, is the untrammelled and undivided power to make laws. It is the supreme power over subjects; 'the right to impose laws generally on all subjects regardless of their consent.[17]

It was Hobbes, however, who was the first to grasp fully the nature of public power as a special kind of institution — an 'Artificial Man', defined by permanence and sovereignty, giving life and motion' to society and body public.'[18]

Further in the words of Fiona Robinson, 'As Peterson and Runyan argue, sovereign men and sovereign states are defined not by connection or relationships but by autonomy in decision-making and freedom from the power of others .Security is understood not in terms of celebrating and sustaining life, but as the capacity to be indifferent to 'others' and, if necessary, to harm them'.(Peterson and Runyan,1993,p.34) By interpreting as indifference what is normally understood as prudent non—intervention ,we begin to highlight a serious moral deficiency of both political liberalism and the so-called morality of the states'.[19]

Notwithstanding the traditional definition of sovereignty and the political compulsions that induced its general acceptance, the political climate in which we find ourselves does not permit its continuance in that form. No doubt, the sovereign bodies within the fixed geographical limits will remain and continue to be acknowledged as such but their absolutism as the supreme law-makers, totally beyond challenge from any corner, has been brought under severe strain.

Sovereignty, the state power and territoriality thus stand today in a more complex relation than in the epoch during which the modern nation-state was forged and the post-war era during which the idea of human rights too hold.

---

[16] Ibid 49.

[17] David Held, *Democracy and the Global Order - From the Modern State to Cosmopolitan Governance*, 1995 (Polity Press), 39.

[18] Ibid 40.

[19] Fiona Robinson , The Limits of a Rights—Based approach to International Ethics in Human Rights in Tony Evans edited ,*Fifty Years on –A re-appraisal*, 1998, (Manchester University Press), 63.

Indeed, globalisation is associated not only with a new 'sovereignty regime' but also with the emergence of powerful new non-territorial forms of economic and political organisation in the global domain, e.g. trans- national social movements, international regulatory agencies, and so on. The modern institution of territorially circumscribed sovereign rule appears somewhat anomalous juxtaposed with the trans-national organization of many aspects of contemporary economic and social life. Globalisation in this account is, therefore, associated with a transformation or to use Ruggie's term, an unbundling of relationship between sovereignty, territoriality and state power.'(Ruggie, 1993; Sassen 1996)[20]

The globalisation which has definite impact on the traditional notion of sovereignty has changed the basic character of those institutions which were hitherto regarded as the foundation of a nation's sovereign independence. Moreover, in the fast changing international atmosphere which is encountering the terrorist and nuclear threats, the global community, if it adheres strictly to the principle of non-intervention on the pretext of the collapsing edifice of sovereignty, the doom of the world is inevitable. Most pertinent in this connection are the following observations of Harold J.Laski,

'The pluralists therefore argued that, however majestic and powerful, the state in fact was only one of many associations in society, that, in experience, there were always limits to its powers, and that those were set by the relation between the purpose the state sought to fulfil and the judgment made by men of that purpose.'[21]

What ,as I think now, was right in the pluralist doctrine, were its conceptions,(1) that a purely legal theory of the state can never form the basis of an adequate philosophy of the state .(2) that the state is, in fact, no more entitled to allegiance than any other association on grounds of ethical right or political wisdom; and (3) that its sovereignty is at bottom, a concept of power made valid by the use of a coercion which, in itself, is morally neutral. Society as a complex whole is pluralistic; the united power of the state which we call sovereignty, that legal right as Bodin put it, to give orders to all and receive orders from none, is made monistic (as in the classical legal theory) by the fact

---

[20] Anthony G. Mc Grew ,Human Rights in a Global Age Corning to Terms with Globalisation, in Tony Evans edited, *Human Rights Fifty Years on — A re-appraisal*, 1998 (Manchester University Press) 193.

[21] Harold J.Laski , above n 14, XI(Introductory Chapter).

that it has behind its will ,on all normal occasions, the coercive power to get its will obeyed.[22]

'When a class- society in this sense is destroyed, the need for the state, as a sovereign instrument of coercion, disappears; in Marx's phrase it "withers away". As that is achieved, both the nature of authority and the law it ordains undergo a fundamental transformation.'[23]

'……..The scale of modern civilisation has made the national and sovereign state an institutional expedient of which the political un-wisdom and moral danger are both manifested.'[24]

The sovereignty of states is seen to be a fiction as soon as they attempt the exertion of their sovereignty. Their wills meet with one another; they can not cut a clear and direct route to their goal. Their wills meet, because their relations grow ever more intimate, and the institutions of the sovereign state fail to express the moral wants of those intimate relations.[25]

There are problems of which the impact upon humanity is too vital for any state to be felt to determine by itself what solution it will adopt. The notion of independent sovereignty, for example, leaves France free to invade Germany when and how she pleases; and the only retort that can be made is either a dissent which does not alter the fact, or a war which destroys civilization. Once we realize that the well-being of the world is, in all large issues, one and indivisible, the co-ordinate determination of them is the primary condition of social peace.[26]

In such an aspect the notion of an independent sovereign state is, on the international side, fatal to the well-being of humanity.[27]

The recent instances of how the international community is mobilised in its crusade against terrorism and the efforts to exert pressures on the nations to avert war, lest it should escalate into nuclear conflagration leading to some cataclysmic destruction, have established this reality that what Hobbes and

[22] Ibid Xl (Introductory Chapter).
[23] Ibid XIII (Introductory Chapter).
[24] Ibid 587.
[25] Ibid 662.
[26] Ibid 65.
[27] Ibid 65.

Austin thought of sovereignty can no longer hold feasible in our contemporary world.

THE STRUCTURAL INGREDIENTS OF SOVEREIGNTY AND ISLAMIC PERCEPTION

'Allah! There is no god but He, - the Living, the Self-subsisting Supporter of all. No slumber can seize Him, nor sleep. His are all things in the Heavens and on earth. Who is thee can intercede in His presence except as He permitted?. He knoweth what (appeareth) to His creatures as Before or After or Behind them. Nor shall they compass aught of His knowledge except as He willeth. His Throne doth extend over the heavens and the earth, and He feeleth no fatigue in guarding and preserving them. For He is the Most High, the Supreme (in glory)'[28]

It is enough, for the moment, to postulate the disappearance of state - sovereignty as the conditions without which the life of reason is impossible to states.[29]

'The developments relating to disruptive nationalism and to the all- affected idea of democracy clearly suggest, then, that important new ideas about the nature of' 'the people' may be emerging.'[30]

The above observations clearly suggest that the theories of 'state-sovereignty' and 'nationalism', despite all the claims regarding their final acceptability, are still not firmly rooted and it appears as if a time has come which is necessitating a fresh definition of these terms. Their traditional meanings and significance have collapsed under the weight of changing circumstances. The Hobbes, Locke, Bentham and Austin's definitions of 'sovereign' and 'sovereignty' might have appealed to reason at the time when the abstractions of natural law had totally confused the juristic approach but now with a radical change in the global circumstances, they are heading towards redundancy. Barry Holden observes on this point,

---

[28] The Holy Qur'an, (Abdullah Yusuf Ali trans.1938), Surah 2- Al- Baqarah, Ayat.255.

[29] Harold J.Laski, *A Grammar of Politics* , Eleventh Impression -1982 (George Allen and Unwin Ltd),65.

[30] Barry Holden ,Democratic theory and The Problem of Global Warming, in Barry Holden Edited *The Ethical Dimensions of Global Change*, First Published Great Britain in 1996 (Macmillan Press Ltd),142.

'The 'sovereign people' came to be identified with the nation and 'until recently at least', has accepted a given world divided into nation-states. But it is now being asked whether, in a changing world, this is any longer 'the given'. There is both a questioning of the presumed coincidence of existing nations and states and some dissolution of the division of the world into watertight compartments.'[31]

He says further,
'However, the fact that the central democratic value — mass control of governmental activity - is re-embodied in this emerging conception gives it a definitive importance such that it can be said to re-define 'the people'. The question of who constitute the people' comes to be answered by reference to a fresh specification of which sections of the masses should do the controlling.'[32]

David Held attributes the emergence of the whole notion of sovereignty to the collapse of the established forms of the authority and it was through this new juristic notion that the vacuum could be filled up. The falling power of the Church in Europe, resulting in the clash of authority between the clergy and the aristocracy made it imperative that some new strategy be invented that should be acceptable to both as the centre of power. He writes;

'Sovereignty became a new way of thinking about an old problem; the nature of power and rule. When established forms of authority could no longer be taken for granted, it was the idea of sovereignty that provided a fresh link between political power and ruler ship. In the struggle between Church, state and community, sovereignty offered an alternative way of conceiving the legitimacy of claims to power.'[33]

The modern concept of sovereignty has had many implications and many writers have tried to deal with them in their own way according to the circumstances in which they lived and, moreover, according to the problems they wanted to address through it. Hobbes had his own way of defining it as Raymond Plant observes;

'Hobbes' account of the nature of the sovereign is concerned to draw conclusions about the necessity of the sort of power the sovereign wields from

31 Ibid 139.
32 Ibid 142.
33 David Held, Democracy *and the Global Order - from the Modern State to Cosmopolitan Governance*, first ed. 1995 (Polity Press), 39.

facts about human desire, particularly the desire for power , and the relationship between individuals which follow from a proper understanding of their nature.'[34]

John Austin who is generally credited with having given one of the most precise and accurate definitions of sovereignty was also motivated by the political situation prevailing in England during his lifetime. His definition has been the most controversial one in the sense that whether the sovereign of his imagination is the absolute law-giver, not controlled by any other consideration. Many jurists conclude that the concentration of all powers in the hands of sovereign, to the exclusion of all other factors, is outside the Austinian hypothesis. For example Roger Cotterrell observes;

'First, Austin does not suggest the sovereign is free of limitations but only legal limitations. Thus positive morality (reflected in public opinion, widespread moral or political expectations and ultimately the threat of rebellions) may provide important constraints. Secondly, most of Austin's discussion of sovereignty relate primarily to the conditions of representative democracies. (Especially Britain and the United States) Thirdly, Austin's concept of delegation by the sovereign is used by him to express the possibility (which has become a reality in most complex modem industrialised societies) of very extensive dispersion of legislative, adjudicative, and administrative authority with the overall hierarchical framework of a centralised state.'

Austin's sovereignty is not a legal but a pre-legal notion. It is the logical correlate of an assumed factual obedience. (Manning 1933: 192,202) It is not "a specified organ" or complex of organs, but it means that individual or collectively at whose pleasure the Constitution is changed or subsists intact. (C.A.W. Manning, 1933:192)[35]

Discussing the views of Rousseau about sovereignty, Martin, J. Walsh observes, it should be observed that the 'sovereign' means, in Rousseau, not the monarch or the government, but the community in its collective and legislative capacity.

'The social contract can be stated in the following words. Each of us puts his person and all his power in common under the supreme direction of the general will, and, in our corporate capacity, we receive each member as an indivisible part of the whole.' This act of association creates a moral and

[34]Raymond Plant, *Modern Political Thought*, 1991(Basil Blackwell), 11.
[35]Roger Cotterrell, *The Politics of Jurisprudence -A Critical Introduction to Legal Philosophy*, 1989, (Butterworths) 70.

collective body, which is called the state' when passive, the 'sovereign when active, and a power' in relation to other bodies like itself'[36]

Making an elaborate observation about the theory of Jean-Jacques Rousseau, Ian Adams observes,

'Jean-Jacques Rousseau (1712-78): His argument was that what distinguishes the human from the animal was not that humans have reason, but the fact that human beings are capable of moral choice and, therefore, men must be free in order to exercise that choice. If people are not free, or if their freedom is restricted, then their humanity is being denied and they are being treated as sub-human, as slaves or animals.'

Rousseau then went on to insist that if people had to live according to laws they did not make themselves, then they are not free, they are slaves. It made little difference if a law-making body had been elected by the people, since it was still other people making the laws; those subject to them were still denied the freedom which was their natural right as human beings. On Rousseau's theory, vast majority of us living in today's liberal democracies are denied their rightful freedom and, therefore, 'slaves'.

If everyone voted according to what they knew was the common good, and not their own interests, then the laws passed would be valid and binding; in obeying them everyone would be free because they would be obeying themselves. These laws would be, as he put it, an expression of the 'GENERAL WILL'.

He only wishes that the GENERAL WILL is always right and that 'the voice of the people is the voice of God'. But apart from these theoretical difficulties, Rousseau's notion of an assembly of all citizens is clearly not possible in modern states....'[37]

Commenting on Rousseau, Bertrand Russell, says, (Jean Jacques Rousseau - 1712-78) The social contract involves that whoever refuses to obey the general will shall be forced to do so. 'This means nothing less than that he will be forced to be free'.......... The conception of being forced to be free' is very metaphysical....'[38]

---

[36] Martin. J. Walsh, *A History of Philosophy*, 1985,(Geoffrey Chapman London), 670.

[37] Ian Adams, *Political ideology today*, 1993, Manchester University Press, 20-21.

[38] Bertrand Russell, *History of Western Philosophy and Its Connection with Political and Social Circumstances From the Earliest Times to the Present Day*, 1955,(George Allen and Unwin London) ,671.

In the wake of the developments that have been taking place, especially after the First World War, which have witnessed the emergence of the written constitutions working with the internal dynamics of law, it appears that the traditional conceptualisation of sovereignty was simply a transitional phase in the legal philosophy. The first such assault on sovereignty came from the Pure Theory of Law as expounded by Hans Kelsen who evaluated legal theory, not in terms of sovereign and its subjects, but as an integrated structure of the hierarchy of norms. Discussing Kelsen, Roger Cotterrell observes,

The pure theory of law dissolves away the state's legitimacy as a potential agency of intolerance. It insists that the state is properly seen as merely the effect of the structure of norms governing the relationships of individual human beings. For Kelsen the doctrine of sovereignty is harmful precisely because it asserts the existence of a supreme entity above law.

Equally, the pure theory of law does its best to dissolve away the nation, as a supreme entity, too. Kelsen argues that the logic of the pure theory leads to the recognition of International law as a single supreme legal system; one in which the norms presented as the basic norms of national or municipal legal system, now appear in a new light as subordinate norms within the international legal order whose validity is ultimately governed by a basic norm of International law.[39]

The great fanfare which marked the advent of the sovereignty, as we presently understand it, is gradually fading away. There was a time when the emergence of the British Parliament as an omnipotent sovereign body was heralded in legal philosophy as a landmark development but now it is being considered as having produced a negative impact on individual freedom F.A. Hayek writes on this development. "The triumphant claim of the British Parliament to have become sovereign, and so able to govern subject to no law, may prove to have been the death-knell of both individual freedom and democracy."[40]

In the context of the sovereign's unlimited powers, Joseph Raz, while quoting Robert Paul Wolff, observes,

---

[39] Roger Cotterrell, *The Politics of Jurisprudence , A Critical Introduction to Legal Philosophy*, 1989, (Butterworths), 115.

[40] F.A. Hayek, New *Studies in Philosophy, Politics, Economics and the History of Ideas,* first published in 1978, 1990 ,(Routledge),154.

'Robert Paul Wolff, to take one well-known example says that authority is the right to command, and correlatively, the right to be obeyed.' (Robert Paul Wolff- In Defence of Anarchism. New York, 1970.p.4)[41]

David Held, while explicating the various structural ingredients of sovereignty, writes, 'The idea of state sovereignty was the source of the idea of impersonal state power. But it was also the legitimating framework of a centralised power system in which all social groups in the long run wanted a stake. How elements of both state and popular sovereignty were to be combined coherently remained far from settled.'[42]

If sovereignty is the rightful capacity to take political decisions and to enact the law within a given community with some degree of finality, it must be entrenched in certain rules and institutions from which it cannot free itself.[43]

CONCLUSION

Coming to Islamic conception, the most important thing is that the concept of sovereignty as inferred from the attributes of Allah bears many similarities to the modern concepts. Not only that, but it appears that Islamic concept is the progenitor of the whole philosophical conceptualisation regarding the definitions of sovereignty. The wordings of *Kalima*:[44] the first declaration of faith- that 'There is no god but Allah and Muhammad is His Messenger bear a strong proximity to the Austinian theory that 'If a determinate human superior, not in the habit of obedience to a like superior' and to Kelsen's theory of' the hierarchy of norms', meaning thereby that the Grundnorm is the justification for all subordinate norms whereas no norm can be used to justify the existence of Grundnorm. It is self-subsisting. All the conceptual aspects of sovereignty, its positive and negative implications, as found in Austin and Kelsen's theories are present in the *Kalima*. The following verses are most relevant to understand the Islamic philosophy of Divine Sovereignty;

41 Joseph Raz, *The Authority of Law - Essays on Law and Morality*, 1979 (Clarendon Press- Oxford), 11.

42 David Held, *Democracy and The Global order from the Modern State to cosmopolitan Governance*, first published – 1995,(Polity Press),46.

43 Ibid 157.

44 Explanation of the word 'Kalima:' There is no god only Allah and Muhammad is the messenger of Allah

'O ye who believe! Spend out of the (bounties). We have provided for you, before the Day comes when no bargaining (will avail), nor friendship, nor intercession. Those who reject Faith, they are the wrong-doers.'[45]

'Allah! There is no God but He, - the Living, the Self-subsisting, Supporter of all. No slumber can seize Him, nor sleep. His are all things in the Heavens and• on earth. Who is thee can intercede in His presence except as He permitteth? He knoweth what (appeareth) to His creatures as Before or After or Behind them. Nor shall they compass aught of His knowledge except as He willeth. His Throne doth extend over the heavens and the earth, and He feeleth no fatigue in guarding and preserving them. For He is the Most High, the Supreme (in glory).'[46]

'Whatever is in the Heavens and on Earth, doth declare the praises and glory of Allah, - the Sovereign, the Holy One, the Exalted in Might, the Wise. It is He Who has sent amongst the unlettered a messenger from among themselves , to rehearse to them His Signs, to purify them, and to instruct them in the Book and Wisdom, - although they had been, before in the manifest error'.[47]

'Whatever is in the heavens and on earth, doth declare the Praises and Glory of Allah: to Him belongs dominion, and to Him belongs praise: and he has power over all things.'[48]

In the present context, it is not only necessary that the existence of the ultimate authority as the last grundnorm must be established but the form of that authority is equally important. The authority, from the viewpoint of the faith may be taken as the Creator or Sustainer of the entire universe, but this aspect of the Authority is not enough to fulfil the need for which we discuss it from the juristic angle. In law the supposition of such an authority assumes a totally different dimension. When in jurisprudence we discuss this concept of authority, we mean the whole range of those attributes which are imperative to dominate human intelligence and rationality while laying down the guidelines for the governance.

---

[45] The Holy Qur'an, (Abdullah Yusuf Ali trans 1938),Surah. 2-Al- Baqarah, Ayat. 254.
[46] *Ibid.* 255.
[47] *Ibid.* Surah, 62- al-Jumuah, Ayat. 1-2.
[48] *Ibid.* Surah, 64- at - Taghabun, Ayat, 1.

Law and Decision Making: Incorporating Internal Harm into Rational Choice Theory

Joshua Masters[1]
New York University

One does not have to experience driving in peak-hour traffic in New Delhi for very long to realize that not all drivers obey traffic laws or rules of tort law. Indeed, in that city at least, those who do appear to be the exception rather than the rule. A road sign that reads "Wearing a helmet could save your life. Law or not", suggests that motorcycle riders require some additional reason for action beyond the law. This raises important questions. Why is the fact that a law is a law not enough to dictate certain behavior for its subjects? How does a legal rule influence an agent's behavior? In other words, when an agent decides whether or not to engage in behavior that may or would impose criminal or tortious liability, to what extent does that law influence the decision? Through the imposition of liability, law demands certain behavior; it creates an obligation. But the obligation of a law is not sufficient to accurately predict an agent's response to it. Laws are often broken. As well as breaking traffic rules, some people murder, or negligently put others at risk, or do not pay taxes. What then explains responses to legal rules? This article endeavors to delineate an explanatory theory of behavior in response to legal rules, as distinct from a normative or predictive theory. The theory modifies the standard rational choice account by treating two distinct causes of internal harm as affecting an agent's well-being.

An agent will have a limited set of possible choices that can be made. There is also a set of potential outcomes that may arise from each of the possible decisions. The agent will have certain beliefs as to the likelihood of each of those outcomes being realized as a result of a given decision. The agent will also have preferences over each of the potential outcomes.[2] Thus, in order to effect a decision, a law must either:

---

[1] B.Ec., University of New England, Australia; LL.B., University of Adelaide; LL.M., New York University School of Law. jdm452@nyu.edu.

[2] See Lewis A. Kornhauser, 'The Normativity of Law' 1(1) *American Law and Economics Review* 3, 7 (1999).

- change the set of possible choices that can be made,
- change the potential outcomes arising from each possible decision,
- change the beliefs of the decision maker as to the likelihood of those outcomes being realized, or
- change the preferences of the decision maker.

The aim of this article is to thoroughly evaluate the basis of claims that law might affect each of these aspects of decision making. Part I considers the effect law has on an agent's choice set. The effect of law on both potential outcomes of behavior and an agent's beliefs about those outcomes is discussed in Part II. The potential for law to change preferences is considered in Part III. Part IV examines the mechanism by which law affects the above aspects of decision-making, namely by providing information to the agent. This article distinguishes between the relationship information has with external outcomes and the relationship it has with internal outcomes. Finally Part V reflects on the ramifications of the theory for the economic analysis of law. While criminal law offers the starkest application of the theory, it is also important to examine its more subtle operation in the context of tort law. Throughout the article, examples from each are used to explain various issues relating to the theory.

While much of this article's analysis of law's effect on behavior agrees with the standard rational choice theory, it concludes that norms have a more significant role to play than that theory allows. However, rather than creating exclusionary reasons, as it is said to do in obligation theory, they are better viewed as creating psychological harm if they are breached, and thereby amount to a mere incentive in the rational choice theory. Such an incentive can be created by law through changing the outcomes of a decision. The rational choice theory is thereby modified to include internal outcomes as incentives. An example of how the theory better predicts behavior is outlined in the final part.

Changing the Choice Set

This Part considers the possibility that law might change the set of choices available to an agent. A choice set is made up of all of the possible actions that an agent could take at a given moment. That is to say, any action that is within the realm of possibility, rather than the actions to which the agent gives serious consideration. Outlining the choice set is of course an important first step in the explanation of an agent's behavior. The behavior of the agent must form part of the possible choices among behavior that are open to the agent. It is difficult to conceptualize the possibility that a law might introduce a behavior into the agent's choice set. Of course, a law might, for example, change the legal status or liability of the agent as a result of certain behavior, but making particular behavior possible that was not possible before is another matter.

It goes without saying that if certain behavior is not available to the agent, then the agent cannot behave in that manner. If the law then could somehow remove a target behavior from an agent's choice set, it would thereby render it impossible for the agent to behave in that way.

Raz's normative theory of behavior includes 'exclusionary reasons' for behavior, which, as the name suggests, exclude reasons for choices from the agent's deliberations.[3] Could that theory be extended such that the obligation of law (at this point we need not distinguish between an obligation to follow the law, and an obligation to follow a particular law) acts to exclude choices from the choice set? For example, if it is illegal for me to cross the street at a set of traffic lights unless the 'walk' signal is lit, then the law would operate to remove the possibility of crossing the street when the light is not lit from my choice set. It is difficult to see that it does so. It is even more difficult to see that a rule imposing liability for negligence removes the possibility that an agent with act negligently. As noted earlier, many people break laws. So for them, the law has not excluded the illegal or tortious action from their choice set. It would be interesting though to consider whether any person might be affected in that way by law. However, even if we imagine an agent who never breaks the law, a 'good' citizen, it does not automatically follow that illegal or tortious actions have been removed from the good citizen's choice set. Consider a lawmaker who wishes to prevent fatalities occurring as a result of negligent operation of a motor-vehicle by attaching liability to such conduct. Even if the good citizen accepts the obligation to drive with due

[3] Joseph Raz, *Practical Reason and Norms* (Oxford University Press, 1975).

caution, we cannot say that it is not possible for her to drive negligently, she has simply chosen not to do so. Consider now a city councilor who does not want citizens to walk on the grass in a park. If the councilor were to pave the grassed area, we would accept that walking on the grass has been removed from the choice set of the citizenry. It is simply no longer possible to walk on the grass, as there is no grass to be walked on. We might also accept that if the councilor were to erect an electrified fence with a 24 hour guard around the grass, then walking on the grass might have been removed from the citizen's (reasonable) choice set. Again, it would not be possible, or reasonably possible, for the citizen to walk on the grass. However, if the councilor instead left the grass intact and unguarded and passed a law making it illegal to walk on the grass, even for the good citizen, we find it difficult to say that the choice of walking on the grass is not available. We would not say that the good citizen has been forced to stay off the grass, but rather that she has chosen to obey the law and stay off the grass.

In that sense, if certain behavior remains theoretically possible, it remains within the agent's choice set. A legal rule cannot, without more, cause certain behavior that was once possible to become impossible, or vice-versa.

Consider now, a Federal government, which passes the Defense of Grass Act, which obliges all metropolitan councils to erect electrified fences with 24 hour guard around the grass. Could we say that the Defense of Grass Act has removed walking on the grass from the choice set of the citizen? We are considering how a legal rule affects the decision making process of the citizen. But in this example, the law has not removed the option of walking on the grass from the choice set. It was not until the obligation of the law, in the form of the fence and guard, was met, that walking on the grass became impossible. It was not the law that changed the choice set, it was the erection of the fence and hiring of the guard. It may be the first link in the causal chain, but does not change the choice set simply by virtue of its existence.

If law cannot change the choice set of an agent, it must affect decisions in a different way. The next Part considers whether a law might affect the potential outcomes of certain behavior, or the beliefs of an agent about the likelihood of those outcomes.

Potential Outcomes and Beliefs

Categories of Outcomes

Before considering whether law can change potential outcomes or the beliefs of an agent, it is useful to categorize the types of outcomes that might be included in the set of potential outcomes. The economic theory of rational behavior holds that only well-being matters to the agent.[4] Outcomes that affect the well-being of the agent are usually thought of as external outcomes. We can distinguish between internal and external outcomes. We might also call these outcomes psychological and non-psychological. An external, or non-psychological outcome is observable by the decision maker, members of a society and an independent observer of a society. Common examples related to the law are taxes, fines, incarceration, civil liability, etc. For example, each of those entities might after a period of observation, expect that a tortfeasor will be sued in a civil court and, if found liable, be required to pay damages, or that a murderer will be arrested by the police, tried in a criminal court, and if convicted, be imprisoned or put to death. Psychological outcomes will not be observable to the independent observer. For example, an independent observer will not, in the absence of the consequences outlined above know that a tortious act or murder is 'wrong'. The wrongdoer may however consider that a tortious act or murder is wrong if he accepts that norm as a guide to his behavior. Breaching that norm will cause some internal harm to the wrongdoer aside from the non-psychological consequences outlined above. The internal harm is not observable to any entity other than the wrongdoer.

[4] See Lewis A. Kornhauser, 'The New Economic Analysis of Law: Legal Rules as Incentives', in *Law and Economics* 27, 42 (Nicholas Mercuro ed.,1989); Lewis A. Kornhauser, 'Interest, Commitment and Obligation: How Law Influences Behavior', in *Justice and Power in Sociological Studies* 208, 215 (Bryant G. Garth and Austin Sarat eds.,1998).

External outcomes might be anything that affects an agent's well-being, and will have different weights assigned to them by different decision makers, depending on their risk aversion and their preferences for the potential outcomes (their utility function). As a simplified example, assume that two people have the same preference for money and also share the same preference for arriving at a destination quickly, the person with lower risk aversion may choose to drive a car at a negligent speed if there is 99% chance of reaching her destination quickly and a 1% chance of causing damage for which she is liable, whereas the person with higher risk aversion might choose to not drive at a negligent speed. Furthermore, if we assume that the two people have equal risk aversion and equal preference for arriving at a destination quickly, the person with a higher preference for money may choose to not drive at a negligent speed, whereas the person with lower preference for money may choose to drive at a negligent speed. The external outcome that might be affected by a law relates to the external incentives created by the law. In the example above, if the law states that a person driving at a negligent speed is liable for any damages caused thereby, the external incentive to accept the obligation created by the law to not drive at a negligent speed is the threat of liability for any damages caused thereby. Of course, the decision maker will also take into account the likelihood of that liability being realized. That likelihood might depend on observing the verdicts in other like cases, the availability of witnesses, the skill of the defense attorney, etc.

Internal outcomes related to a law may be divided into two categories. The first, relates to the norm that overlaps the subject matter of the law. The second relates to the norm that the law should be obeyed. These internal outcomes depend upon the agent's acceptance or commitment to those rules.[5] If the agent does accept them, then an outcome of breaching a legal rule will be internal harm. A harm resulting from not following the subject matter norm, or, a harm resulting from not following the law because it is a law. The harm is related to an agent's conscience. For example, if an agent thinks that people should always tell the truth and the agent

[5] See Kornhauser's discussion of HLA Hart, 'The Normativity of Law', supra note 1.

lies, she feels bad because she has breached a norm which she subscribes to; she has suffered an internal harm.

It is worth considering whether the normative obligation to obey the law exists at all. In the context of a just government, the legal obligation to obey the law is said by Raz to appear to depend on the existence of an independent legal obligation (moral duties as he calls them), to obey each of the laws of the system.[6] However, a normative obligation to obey the law creates an apparent paradox. Raz uses the example of murder to illustrate the paradox in terms of morality. The same might be said in terms of normativity. There is a normative obligation not to murder. But to refrain from murder simply because of a normative obligation to obey a law that prohibits murder is not a normatively correct reason to do so. The paradox states that it cannot be normatively incorrect to follow a normative obligation. However, as Raz notes, that type of paradox is overstated. There may be an obligation to follow laws in certain circumstances. It is not the case that if there are certain laws where there is no obligation to obey, then there is never an obligation to obey a law beyond an obligation related to the subject matter of the law. Raz provides examples of circumstances where there is an obligation to obey the law simply because it is law as situations where the judgment of government experts is better than the agent; where the government is better able to end a widespread and damaging practice; and where non-compliance will undermine the government's ability to do good.

In my view, the paradox is not merely overstated, but is, rather, illusory. That is particularly so if there is a normative obligation to follow all laws rather than a separate obligation to follow some individual laws. An agent can have a normative obligation to not murder and also have a normative obligation to follow the law, which includes the prohibition of murder. Each normative obligation offers a reason for action to the agent. Choosing to not meet one or the other of those obligation would have the outcome of causing internal harm to any agent who subscribed to those norms. It is too simplistic to say that choosing to not commit murder solely because it is against the law is normatively incorrect. In that example, we see at least two decisions. The first is to not use a normative obligation to refrain from murder as a reason to not

[6] Joseph Raz, *Ethics in the Public Domain* 326-327 (Oxford: Clarendon Press,1994).

murder. The second is to meet the normative obligation to follow the law. The first decision is normatively incorrect. The second decision is normatively correct. We might say that if the agent has a higher preference for meeting the first obligation than the second, then, on weighing the two aspects of the decision, on balance the decision was normatively incorrect. However, if the agent had a higher preference for meeting the normative obligation to follow the law than for meeting the normative obligation to refrain from murder, then the decision was, on balance, normatively correct. Of course, it is inherently appealing to accept that the normative obligation to not murder has greater weight than any normative obligation to follow the law. That causes the illusory paradox to be, on its face, appealing.

Thus, there are at least some circumstances (if the paradox is overstated), if not all (if the paradox is illusory), where there is an internal obligation to obey the law because it is a law, and a corresponding harm that is suffered if that obligation is not met by an agent recognizing the obligation.

The existence of a normative obligation to obey the law is best illustrated by the comparison of laws that permit behavior and laws that prohibit it. If a parking space is allocated through the use of a parking meter that charges a fixed amount, an agent will decide whether to park there based solely on external matters, including the costs and benefits of parking and paying the fee to her well-being. If, on the other hand, parking was prohibited in that space, and a sanction is in place equal to the fixed charge, we would expect less people to park in the space. This does not suggest that the law has acted as an exclusionary reason for acting (because parking remains possible), but rather that, external costs remaining equal, the internal harm caused by not following the law is an additional cost to be taken into account by the agent.

An interesting challenge to the idea of internal harm is posed by the consideration of the actions of corporations in similar permission/prohibition examples. If corporations treat fines and taxes differently, then the theory that individuals only do so because of a psychological harm is weakened. If corporations have no personality outside of their legal personality, how can a corporation suffer psychological harm? If corporations do indeed treat permissive taxes and prohibitive fines differently, then it must be some other consideration that affects their behavior.

The possibility that a corporation would treat these types of incentives differently, might be explained in two ways. First, if the corporation breaks the law, its standing in the community will be damaged and so profits may be affected. Thus the behavior is a reaction to external outcomes. However, internal outcomes might also operate to affect their behavior. It is an individual or individuals who ultimately make the decision on behalf of the company as to whether or not it should break the law. In that circumstance, the behavior of the company is affected by the internal harm that the individual(s) would suffer. The harm may be diluted by the individual's removal from responsibility for the behavior, but may be there nonetheless.

In any event, it is not clear that corporations do treat permissive taxes and prohibitive penalties differently. The legal community has long understood that corporations, particularly large corporations, may treat fines as simply another cost of doing business.[7] If that is the case, then no damage is caused to the theory of internal harm suffered as a result of breaking a law because it is a law. In any event, to the extent that any corporation does treat them differently, that treatment has been explained in a consistent manner above.

Internal outcomes are not usually considered to affect an agent's well-being. That is where the legal and economic theories of behavior in response to law differ.[8] However, the distinction between, for example, physical or pecuniary harm on the one hand, and internal harm on the other, is unnecessary for the purposes of identifying outcomes that affect an agent's well-being. If that distinction is removed, the economic theory is capable of processing internal harm.

---

[7] See, e.g., New South Wales Law Reform Commission, Sentencing: Corporate Offenders, Issues Paper No 20 (2001) [3.9]; John C. Coffee, Jr., "No Soul to Damn: No Body to Kick": An Unscandalized Inquiry Into the Problem of Corporate Punishment, 79 MICH. L. REV. 386 (1980–1981); Linda S. Bosniak, 'Exclusion and Membership: The Dual Identity of the Undocumented Worker under United States Law', 1988 Wisconsin Law Review 955,1015 (1988). Cf, Kornhauser, 'Interest, Commitment, and Obligation', supra note 3.

[8] See Kornhauser, 'The Normativity of Law', supra note 1.

Having explored the different types of outcomes that face an agent, namely, external and internal outcomes, this article now considers whether law can change the outcomes that an agent might face, or the agent's beliefs as to the likelihood that such outcomes will occur.

Changing Outcomes and Beliefs

As a result of a decision by an agent, a certain outcome will occur. Different decisions may lead to different outcomes. However each decision has only one inevitable outcome. That outcome is made up of an almost infinite number of individual consequences. For example, if I choose to cross a street, individual consequences might be that I step in a puddle, am beeped at by a car, and make it to the other side quicker than I would have if I had chosen to cross the street at a later time. In a certain world, an agent will know the exact consequences of a decision, and so, will choose the decision that results in the most preferred outcome. However, the world is not certain. An agent is only able to identify consequences which she considers possible results of her decision, which may or may not include the consequences that make up the inevitable outcome. Thus, for each possible choice in an agent's choice set, there is a set of subjectively potential outcomes. Corresponding with the subjectively potential outcomes of each of the choices is a belief of the agent as to the likelihood that each potential outcome will occur. That in turn depends on the agent's belief as to the likelihood of certain consequences occurring. For example, consider a jurisdiction where the voluntary assumption of risk is a complete bar to recovery of damages in tort. If I decide to cross the street while there is a 'do not walk' sign lit, I may have beliefs about the likelihood that I will make it to the other side of the street safely. I may also have beliefs about the likelihood that I would be found by a court to have voluntarily assumed the risk of injury if I do not make it to the other side safely. If I think that there is a 50% chance of each occurring, then I will have the following beliefs about the likelihood of outcomes: 50% chance that I will make it to the other side safely; 25% chance that I will not make it safely to the other side and will not be found to have voluntarily assumed the risk of injury; 25% chance that I will not make it to the other side safely and will be found to have voluntarily assumed the risk of injury. Of course, this simplifies matters in many ways. Not least because the occurrence of one consequence might affect the chance of another consequence occurring.[9] Regardless, the example helps to illustrate how beliefs are compiled.

It was stated earlier that outcomes may be external or internal. On an objective level, we might conclude that law cannot possibly change the potential external outcomes of a decision. Legal rules can be thought of as coercive orders.[10] The coercion may be a result of authority or of threat of punishment. Whatever form an order takes, it does not change what is physically possible and what is not. It may not be likely that a police officer will arrest me for selling apples if selling apples is legal, but it is possible. There is nothing to physically restrain the police officer from doing so. If the law made selling apples a criminal offence, it has not done anything to make my arrest physically possible. It has, however, merely made it more likely, assuming that the police officer obeys the command of the law and thus is inclined to enforce the law by arresting those who commit criminal offences. Thus, we might conclude that, on an objective level, the law does not affect the set of potential external outcomes.

Internal outcomes are another matter. In particular, a normative obligation to follow a law because it is law will indeed create a potential outcome, even at an objective level. Choosing to undertake behavior that will now be contrary to law, where it was not before, will have a new outcome: the harm caused internally to the agent by not meeting the normative obligation to follow the law. So we see that law can change the objective set of potential outcomes by the creation of new normative obligations. The use of the word potential is perhaps not necessary in this context. An agent either subscribes to a norm or not. If the agent does subscribe to a norm, then breaching it will definitely cause an internal harm. If the agent does not breach the norm, it will definitely not cause an internal harm. These are not situations where the agent will have varying

---

[9] It is also unlikely that a pedestrian would consider rules of tort before deciding how careful to be crossing the street: See Gary T. Schwartz, 'Reality in the Economic Analysis of Tort Law: Does Tort Law Really Deter?' 42 *UCLA Law Review* 377, 429 (1994).

[10] H.L.A. Hart, *The Concept of Law* 20-25 (Oxford: Clarendon Press, 1961) .

beliefs about the likelihood of those outcomes occurring. It is more interesting when considering situations where the agent is unsure as to whether a norm will be followed or not as a result of certain behavior. The uncertainty itself acts to mitigate any internal harm that is suffered should the agent reach the conclusion later than a norm was breached. Nonetheless, the agent is bound to suffer a greater internal harm if later it is concluded that a norm was breached, than if a norm was not breached. The uncertainty only mitigates, rather than removes, the harm. Thus, we might conclude that in circumstances where there is uncertainty about whether or not a norm will be breached, then the outcome remains uncertain to the agent.

The agent is concerned only with those outcomes of each possible choice that are foreseeable to the agent. Limitations of cognitive ability mean those outcomes are unlikely to be coincident with the set of objectively possible outcomes. The subjective nature of the definition of the set of potential outcomes might allow us to depart from the objective conclusion that law cannot affect that set. A decision is based only on foreseeable outcomes. Equally, unforeseeable individual outcomes play no role in the agent's deliberation. I say individual outcomes because an agent may give consideration to the potential for unforeseeable outcomes generally. (Rumsfeld's unknown unknowns). What is it then that makes an outcome foreseeable? In the common law world, a foreseeable event is an event that is not 'far-fetched or fanciful'[11]. Even an event which has an infinitesimal chance of occurring is foreseeable.[12] In the High Court of Australia, Mason J (as he then was) has stated: 'Although it is true to say that in many cases the greater the degree of probability of the occurrence of the risk the more readily it will be perceived to be a risk, it certainly does not follow that a risk which is unlikely to occur is not foreseeable'. Of course, a court necessarily must describe an objective account of forseeability, usually, based on some standard of the reasonableness. That necessity exists because only the agent will actually know what was and was not foreseen by her. A court has the task of describing a normative account of what should have been foreseen. Nevertheless, the likelihood of occurrence forms the basis of objective and subjective accounts of

[11] *Wyong Shire Council v. Shirt* (1980) 146 C.L.R. 140 (Australia).
[12] *Bolton v. Stone* [1951] UKHL 2 (U.K.).

what is foreseeable. We might conclude then that whether an outcome is foreseeable or not depends on the likelihood of its occurrence. There must be some real chance of it occurring in order for the outcome to be foreseeable. Pursuant to that test, my arrest for selling apples if selling apples is legal is unforeseeable because it is in my mind fanciful. I do not think there is a real chance of it occurring.

Thus, the set of foreseeable outcomes are defined by the agent's beliefs about the likelihood of a decision leading to a particular outcome. An outcome will be foreseeable and thus within the agent's subjective set of potential outcomes if the agent believes that its occurrence reaches a certain (very low) threshold of likelihood. A potential outcome that is too unlikely will be unforeseeable and thus not included in the weighing deliberations of the agent. It is not that such an outcome is considered and discarded as too unlikely, but rather, it is so unlikely that it does not enter the mind of the agent at all. Thus, for law to affect an agent's decision by changing the set of potential outcomes, it must either remove or introduce an outcome into the realm of forseeability of the agent.

So, for the purposes of the agent's decision making process, the set of potential outcomes is defined by subjective measures. If a legal rule can change the beliefs of the agent, then the agent's set of subjective potential outcomes may also be changed. Consider the sale of apples example again. I must decide whether or not to sell apples. If selling apples is legal, then, even though it is physically possible that I could be arrested by a police officer for selling apples, it is so unlikely, that it is not a foreseeable outcome of a decision to sell apples. The chance that it will happen is so insignificant that the possibility of it will not enter my mind at all. Thus, in my deliberations, I will not place any weight on the possibility that I could be arrested. If selling apples was made a criminal offense, and I was made aware of that information, that I might be arrested by a police officer is now likely enough that the possibility of that outcome enters my mind as a foreseeable result of selling apples. Consequently, my decision may be affected, depending on my preference for not being arrested and the weight given to other considerations.

I noted above that possible outcomes identified by the agent may not include the inevitable outcome, either because the inevitable outcome was far-fetched, or because the agent has mistakenly overlooked a potential outcome. In an uncertain world, the agent does not know the inevitable outcome. Consequently, whether or not a law affects the inevitable outcome is not necessarily of any consequence in the agent's decision-making process.

The agent's beliefs about the likelihood of particular outcomes are informed by information that is available to the agent. Uncertainty is a result of imperfect information. Therefore, on the assumption that law cannot change what is physically possible, in order for a legal rule to change the forseeability of an event, and thus introduce it or remove it from the set of potential outcomes of an agent, it must do so by changing the information available to the agent.

Of course, an agent's behavior may also be affected by a law that changes an agent's beliefs about the likelihood of an outcome that is already within their set of potential outcomes. For example, consider the difference between a comparative negligence regime and a contributory negligence regime. In a comparative negligence regime, a plaintiff is barred from recovery of damages if her own negligence is deemed to have contributed a certain amount to the cause of those damages, say 50% or more. In a contributory negligence regime, a plaintiff is barred from recovery of damages if her negligence is found to have contributed to the cause of those damages at all. If I were a particularly contemplative person and drove a car in low visibility with slightly worn brakes, I might consider the likelihood of my being barred from recovery of damages if I were involved in a crash with a car driving on the wrong side of the road without lights. In a comparative negligence regime, I might believe that there was a small likelihood that I would be barred from recovery of damages. However, if the regime were changed to contributory negligence, then I would believe that there was a greater likelihood of being barred from recovery of damages. That change in belief may change my choice to drive even though it has not introduced or removed the potential outcome of being barred from recovery from my set of potential outcomes.

So whether it changes the set of potential outcomes or not, the law can affect an agent's behavior by changing the agent's beliefs about the likelihood of potential outcomes. A law can do this by creating new information, or by bringing existing information to the agent's attention. How a legal rule might do this is explored below in Part IV. Before that, I consider whether the law might affect an agent's behavior by changing the agent's preferences.

Changing Preferences

The preferences of an agent rank outcomes. In a certain world, an agent will prefer the inevitable outcome of one decision to the inevitable outcome of another decision. In an uncertain world, preference cannot be simply reduced to a preference for the outcome of one decision over the outcome of another. In an uncertain world, the set of subjectively potential outcomes for each decision are ranked. Then the agent will combine preferences over the potential outcomes, beliefs as to likelihood of occurrence, and her risk aversion, to obtain an all things considered conclusion. As discussed above, normative obligation is incorporated in this calculation through the inclusion of internal harm as an outcome over which an agent has preference.

As it was with the choice set, it is difficult to conceptualize how a law might change the preference of an agent. If, in a given circumstance, I prefer x over y, how can a law result in my preferring y over x in the same circumstances? If a motorcyclist prefers the feeling of driving with no helmet, can a law result in the motorcyclist preferring the feeling of wearing a helmet?

There are three claims that might be made as to how law could change the preferences of an agent. First, if a law forms habits in the agent, those habits might lead to a change in preference. For example, if I dislike wearing a helmet, but wear it for a period of time because I may be barred from recovery of damages if I do not, I may grow to like the feeling of wearing a helmet. Then even if that threat is removed, say by the negligence regime changing from contributory to comparative or pure comparative negligence, I continue to wear the helmet because I am used to the feeling, and perhaps prefer the warmth or feeling of safety that it offers. The strength of this claim is undermined by its causal relationship. On the first day of application of a rule that would bar recovery of damages for not wearing a helmet, the law has had no effect on my preference for wearing a helmet. It is at best an indirect effect on my preferences. The distinction is important particularly if the explanatory theory is to have any application in a design project. If the change in preference requires me to wear the helmet consistently over time, then the other effects of law must be the sole consideration in design of a law that will cause me to do that in the first place. For example, the primary, or direct, effects of law, such as changing beliefs through the provision of information, is required before any effect on my preference can be effected. Nonetheless, habituation makes the best claim as to how the law can change preferences. It is important to note that the habit does not simply change my preference for the behavior that the law encourages. The habit must change my preference for one or more of the outcomes of the behavior. In the helmet example, I might have changed my preference for the feeling that I get when wearing a helmet, rather than a preference for wearing the helmet. If it were otherwise, that would confuse my decision with my preferences.

The second claim relates to the normativity of law. If law is respected by the agent as a norm, it will alter her motivations in some significant way. The claim might be, for example, that if my religious beliefs require me to protect my head by wearing a helmet at all times, then my preference for wearing helmets will change. Similarly, if the law is accepted as a norm, it too will change my preference by altering my motivations. In my view, however, this simply confuses preference changing with changing the set of outcomes. If I accept the wearing of a helmet as a norm, I wear it, at least in part, to avoid the internal harm from not abiding by the norm. That says nothing about whether I nonetheless prefer the feeling of not wearing a helmet.

The third claim is that the law can change preferences through the provision of certain types of information. For example, if the law were able to provide me with the information that helmets improve my safety, the feeling of wearing a helmet might change from being a feeling of discomfort, to a feeling of safety, thus changing my preference for the feeling of wearing a helmet compared to not. However, this claim too appears to suffer from confusion as to the true underlying change. It may be that the information simply changes my beliefs about the likelihood that I will suffer significant damage if I ride a motorcycle while wearing a helmet. My preference for the feeling of wearing a helmet to not wearing a helmet has been confused with my decision to wear the helmet or not to wear the helmet.

So, we see that preferences might only be changed indirectly by law, by causing habits to be formed by those who decide to abide by the law for other reasons.[13] Once the preference is changed, the other effects of the law are of less importance in affecting behavior.

Law and Information

It was found above that to affect an agent's behavior, a law must change the information available to the agent, which must change the beliefs of the agent about the likelihood of a potential outcome occurring. This may or may not introduce a potential outcome into the subjective set of potential outcomes of the agent. Over time, if those changes are able to form a habit of the agent to behave in the way the law requires, then the agent's preferences for certain outcomes related to that behavior may also change. To understand how the law might change the information available to the agent, consideration of the categories of outcomes for which the likelihood beliefs of the agent might change, that were outlined above, is important. That will enable us to consider the type of information that might affect those beliefs.

Information and External Outcomes

Sanctions are the most obvious way to change information available to an agent concerning external outcomes. A law describing certain behavior and outlining the liability that will be incurred for undertaking that behavior provides the agent with the information that the behavior may lead to liability of a certain type. The existence of the law is one type of information. The agent will know that the law's existence will make it more likely that legal mechanisms will be implemented to either stop her from continuing that behavior

[13] But cf Kornhauser, 'The New Economic Analysis of Law', supra note 3, 44.

and/or to punish her for it in the way specified in the law. The size of the sanction is important information. The agent will usually prefer a smaller sanction over a larger sanction. Therefore, a larger sanction will be given greater weight in the agent's deliberation and is thus more likely to change the agent's behavior. This type of information is one that not only changes the beliefs and subjective set of outcomes of the agent, it also probably affects the inevitable outcome of the decision. To be effective, the law must adequately define the behavior subject to the law, the obligation, and the sanction.

The law can also provide information that will assist the agent to make a better informed decision. This relates to external outcomes in a different way to sanctions. For example, a law may require the road traffic authority to publish information about the safety benefits of helmets. This type of information will act to change the beliefs and possibly the subjective set of outcomes of the agent. It will not however, have any effect on the inevitable outcome of a decision. For example, if I now know that a helmet is capable of saving my life in a crash, that does nothing to make the wearing of helmets more of less safe. Of course, this type of effect on behavior is secondary in nature, which raises certain problems discussed later. If I choose to wear a helmet as a result of the information, that is a result primarily of the authority reacting to the law, rather than in direct response to the law itself.

Either of those types of information change the beliefs of an agent, and potentially change her set of subjective potential outcomes, and, if habit forming, her preferences over the set of subjective potential outcomes.

Information and Internal Outcomes

It was found above that two types of internal outcomes relate to behavior that may break a law. Psychological harm suffered by not following a norm that overlaps with the subject matter of the law, and psychological harm suffered by not following the norm that the law should be followed.

The information provided by law relating to the second type of internal outcome is that the behavior required by the norm now extends to the subject matter of the law in question. In other words, the norm that I should follow the law has subject matter that equates to subjects dealt with by the law. That subject matter will change as laws change. A new law on subject matter not previously dealt with by law will inform an agent that the norm now covers that subject. The agent already knows that not following that norm will cause internal harm, assuming she subscribes to the norm, and so will now believe with certainty that internal harm will be caused if she behaves in the manner now prohibited. For this result, the law merely needs to set out the subject matter and the obligation. A sanction is not required.

Information provided by the law might also relate to the first type of internal outcome, that is, the harm suffered by the agent when not following a norm that is coincident with the subject matter of the law. It can do this if a law can lead to the creation of a norm covering the subject matter of the law. That is, a norm that would continue to exist without the law itself. A thorough discussion of norm creation is beyond the scope of this paper, however, it might for example occur as a result of the enactment of a law because of the symbolic value of the law.[14] The relation, even if it did exist, however, is secondary. The information must be information of the type(s) discussed above in order to change behavior through either external means or by the extension of the subject matter covered by the norm that the agent should follow the law. Like in the formation of habits, the process must be initiated by a direct change in behavior by the law.

Ramifications for Economic Analysis of Law

We have seen that law can affect behavior by changing beliefs, which may also create new subjective potential outcomes if those outcomes are not already within the agent's set of subjective potential outcomes. Law may also create an inevitable outcome where the agent subscribes to the norm that the law should be

[14] See, e.g., Shubha Ghosh, 'Where's the Sense in *Hill v Gateway 2000*?: Reflections on the Visible Hand of Norm Creation', 26 *Touro Law Review* 1125, 1129 (1999-2000).

followed. This may change behavior as a result of internal harm that an agent would suffer if she breached that norm. Indirectly, the law might change behavior through the creation of new norms that coincide with the subject matter of the law, such that the norms would remain in the absence of the law, which in turn create new inevitable outcomes; or through the formation of habit, which can in turn change the preferences of the agent.

Drawbacks for the Predictive Project

Attempts to use this explanatory theory to predict behavior will encounter difficulties in at least three areas: quantifying internal harm, predicting secondary effects, and irrationality.

Quantifying Internal Harm

While the quality of response to internal effects of law are easy to establish, their quantity is more difficult to predict or measure. Measurement of the effect of sanctions is a task that is familiar to an economist. However, the internal harm suffered as a result of not complying with a norm is more difficult to quantify. Cooter suggests that the harm can be equated with the intrinsic value of obeying a law.[15] In his view, the decision as to whether or not to obey the law is dependent on three measures: the net cost of obeying the law, the net cost of disobeying the law and the agent's willingness to pay to obey the law. In other words, he measures the internal harm suffered by an agent by the amount of money the agent is willing to pay to avoid it. The last measure thus converts the internal harm caused by breaking the law into a monetary value. However, Cooter thus ignores the operation of two distinct types of internal harm, that which results from the existence of two separate norms discussed above. By condensing internal harm to a single measure, the effect of the law is mixed with the internal harm that would have been suffered in any event from an agent not following the norm which coincides with the subject matter of the law. It would be difficult, if not impossible for an agent to separate her willingness to

[15] Robert Cooter, 'The Intrinsic Value of Obeying a Law', 75 *Fordham Law Review* 1275 (2006-2007).

pay to follow the norm that she should not negligently maintain lighting in a stairwell because it is a law from her willingness to pay to follow the norm that she should not negligently maintain lighting in a stairwell because it is wrong. How then, can we measure the effect that law has on an agent through its creation of the outcome of an internal harm?

It is possible, if we continue the assumption that the norm that individuals should follow laws because they are laws does not attach itself to each law individually, but rather to a body of law as a whole. If that holds, then the internal harm will be identical for each law. All that is required then to measure that harm is a law, the subject of which does not coincide with any other norm subscribed to by the agent. An agent's willingness to pay to follow that law will be the equivalent of that agent's internal harm that would be suffered as a result of breaking a law because it is a law. Of course, the internal harm related to a subject matter norm could be calculated by asking the same question of the agent concerning a law, the subject of which does coincide with the other norm. The second type of internal harm will be the difference between the two willingness to pay figures.

For example, imagine a new law that says that citizens should wear blue wigs on Fridays, and there is then no pre-existing norm of that content. Agent A is willing to pay x dollars to follow that law. There is also an old law that says that citizens should wear red hats on Saturdays, which coincides with a norm in society that red hats should be worn on Saturdays (perhaps because that law has existed for long enough to create the norm). A is willing to pay y dollars to follow that law, where following that law will also have the effect that A meets the obligation of the subject matter norm. In that example, the internal harm suffered by A should she not follow any law is x. The total internal harm suffered by A if she does not wear a red hat on Saturday is y. The internal harm suffered by A because she did not follow the norm of wearing a red hat on Saturdays (rather than because it is law) would be y-x.

Another problem raised by Cooter is that some outcomes are incommensurate with money, which is usually the common measure used by economists.[16] This incommensurability might be the result

16 Ibid.

of practical or theoretical problems. The practical problem is that the measure requires agents to identify the amount of money they are willing to pay for a given outcome. That measure is obviously limited by the wealth of the agent. For example it makes little sense for an agent with total wealth of $1,000 to say that they are prepared to pay $10,000 for a given outcome. Cooter states that willingness to pay only measures value so far as an agent is able to pay. However, that limitation might be overcome by asking not how much an agent is willing to pay, but rather, how much they would have to be paid in order for them to be willing to not follow the law.

The theoretical problem raised by Cooter is that there are intrinsic reasons why some goods cannot be given a monetary value. Death, disfigurement, loss of reputation and permanent injury are offered as examples of such goods. However, in the context of the explanatory theory, this problem does not apply. The only effect of law to which this problem could conceivably apply is the internal harm suffered when not following the norm that the law should be obeyed. However, the fact that many people break the law suggests that the internal harm is small enough to be commensurable with money. Even if some people do treat that norm as an exclusory reason for decision, and as such, no amount of money could compensate them for breaching that norm, the problem does not appear to affect the explanatory or predictive project. Indeed, it seems to make prediction far easier. If an infinite weight is placed on the avoidance of that harm, then any set of outcomes where the norm is not breached is preferred to any set of outcomes where the norm is breached. In such situations, the behavior of the individual is predicted with perfect accuracy. Problems might arise however, where two or more outcomes are incommensurable. If that were to occur and the outcomes always acted in the opposite direction, then predictions using the willingness to break the law test are unhelpful.

Predicting Secondary Effects

Further difficulties in the use of this explanatory theory for prediction occur when considering measurement of the indirect effects of law on behavior: providing information for better informed decisions, preference changing through the formation of habits and norm creation. Each requires the passage of significant time, which makes prediction less accurate. Of course, the necessity for the passage of time creates complexities, but so does the secondary nature of law as the cause of the behavior.

One difficulty caused by the secondary effects is the dilutive effect of removal from the law itself. The efficiency of law's influence will dissipate as the agent is removed from the law. If a law in its primary application is unsuccessful in changing behavior in the manner intended, then its indirect, or secondary influence is less predictable.

Of course, the change in behavior accorded to the primary influence of a law will also be unpredictable to the extent that the predictive project is imperfect, but those inaccuracies will be magnified as the distance between law and agent increases. It seems that those magnified inaccuracies can only be removed if an assumption is made that individuals will do as the law says. However, such an assumption is unrealistic. Thus, any prediction based on the formation of habit or creation of norms is bound to be inaccurate on some level.

Irrationality

Furthermore, an agent will not necessarily act rationally. Conduct may be pursued that does not, or does not appear, to be in the best interests of the agent. While it is tempting to disregard such conduct as simply irrational, such conduct may instead point to a gap in our theory of rational behavior. By way of example, Sobel has considered the destructive behavior of fired employees, which does not appear to be in their material interest.[17] He suggests that such behavior might be explained in many rational ways if we do not require the employee to be in pursuit of maximum monetary income. One such explanation is that such an employee might attempt to maximize a utility function that depends not only on his own income, but also that of his employer. By damaging the employer's income, the employee increases his own utility.

Of course, to some extent, complete rationality is not possible due to limited access to information or limited computational abilities of

[17] Joel Sobel, 'Interdependent Preferences and Reciprocity', 43 *Journal of Economic Literature* 392.

agents.[18] To compensate, an agent may apply approximations, or 'rules of thumb'. Such rules will not always arrive at the best decision possible, but may produce better decisions on average over time than random decisions, or lead to a more desirable outcome than would obtained if the agent spent sufficient time to gather the necessary information and making calculations.

The explanative theory will be unhelpful in predicting individual circumstances where behavior appears irrational. However, unless agents are consistently or often irrational, irrationality causes less significant problems for the theory than the other difficulties described above. In particular, irrationality will be less significant in predicting average effects of laws on behavior than the potential difficulties associated with quantification of internal harm and prediction of secondary or indirect effects. Irrational agents may react to laws in a way that causes some behavioral outliers, the significance of which are negated upon aggregation with the behavior of all affected agents.[19]

Improvements made by the theory

The theory takes ideas from the obligation theory (the idea that norms create exclusionary reasons for action) and incorporates them into the rational choice theory, by viewing obligations as creating the potential for internal harm. That harm is ranked alongside other outcomes as a preference of the agent. Indeed, agents who do behave as the obligation theory predicts might simply be said to suffer such great psychological harm when breaching a norm, that the avoidance of such harm is always preferred and thus outweighs other reasons for action. The theory is also better at explaining why an apparent obligation resulting from one norm might be overcome by another; a breach of each norm causes different levels of psychological harm, which might be weighed against one another and the other outcomes to find a preference.

[18] See Herbert A. Simon, 'A Behavioral Model of Rational Choice', 69 *Quarterly Journal of Economics* 99.
[19] See Gary S. Becker, 'Irrational Behavior and Economic Theory', 70 *Journal of Political Economy* 1, 13.

To illustrate, I will use the example of a driver approaching a red traffic light. First, imagine the driver is taking her father, who has suffered a heart attack, to hospital. She knows that the quicker she arrives at the hospital, the more likely her father is to survive. She is under a normative obligation to arrive at the hospital as quickly as possible. At the time, other cars are approaching the intersection perpendicular to the driver and face a green light. Nonetheless, the driver speeds through the red light, narrowly avoiding the other cars, in order to arrive at the hospital earlier than she would if she had waited for a green light or for the other cars to pass. We see here an example of competing normative obligations. On one hand, the driver is obligated to get her father to hospital as quickly as possible, on the other, the driver has a normative obligation to other drivers to drive safely. Furthermore, the driver has an obligation to follow the law, which includes driving with due care and stopping at a red light (in the circumstances, the subject matter of the law overlaps with the normative obligation to drive safely). The driver's external considerations include the possibility of a fine for driving through a red light, the possibility of crashing, being held liable for damages suffered by other drivers and causing herself and her father injury, and the effect that her father's eventual fate will have on her well-being.

In this example, the standard rational choice theory does not take into account the potential for internal harm that is caused by driving negligently and not stopping at the red light. However, in light of the driver's decision to drive negligently and go through the red light, the consequences for predicting her behavior were slight. However, the consequences become more obvious as the degree of emergency decreases. Before considering those situations however, it is worth noting that the explanatory theory outlined in this paper is better able to explain the decision in the face of competing normative obligations than the obligation theory. The driver would simply suffer a greater internal harm by not meeting the obligation to get her father to hospital as quickly as possible than she suffered by driving negligently and proceeding through the red light, thereby breaking the law and not driving in a safe manner. Thus she has a greater preference for the internal outcomes associated with driving negligently and proceeding through the red light than not doing so. That preference is so high that it has also outweighed the potential external outcomes and the competing normative obligations, which would cause different internal harm.

Now consider the situation as the level of emergency decreases, for example, if the driver's father was suffering from a non-life threatening injury, or if she was simply running late for a flight, or for work, or merely wanted to shorten her daily commuting time. Over the range of these circumstances, as we attempt to predict the effect of the law prohibiting a driver from driving negligently or from proceeding through a red light, we expect the standard rational choice theory to underestimate the effect of the law, as it will ignore the potential for internal harm, instead focusing on external considerations such as a potential fine or tortious liability. As such there will be a range of emergency where the standard rational choice theory will predict that the driver will drive negligently and proceed through the red light, when in fact she does not because of her reluctance to suffer the internal harm associated with not following a law. The explanatory theory outlined in this paper will better predict her behavior by allowing for the avoidance of that internal harm as an additional incentive.

Conclusion

This article sets out a theory of the manner in which law can affect human behavior. However, the explanatory theory described holds significant difficulties for those wishing to use it as the basis for a predictive theory. The complexity of the issues involved and uncertainties created by such issues as internal harm, secondary effects and irrationality suggest that a predictive project would need to further improve the explanatory theory. Nonetheless, it should offer better results than the standard rational choice account by incorporating the effects of internal incentives, otherwise ignored by the standard rational choice theory as not relating to well-being.

Acknowledgments: The author wishes to thank Professor Lewis A. Kornhauser (New York University School of Law) for his helpful comments on an earlier draft of this article. The author retains responsibility for any errors or inadequacies remaining.

Made in the USA
Monee, IL
05 November 2026

67814336R00079